A Seeking Heart

REDISCOVERING TRUE WORSHIP

ALICIA WILLIAMSON & SARAH GROVES

A Seeking Heart

REDISCOVERING TRUE WORSHIP

ALICIA WILLIAMSON & SARAH GROVES

New Hope® Publishers
Birmingham, Alabama

New Hope® Publishers
P.O. Box 12065
Birmingham, AL 35202-2065
www.newhopepubl.com

Library of Congress Cataloging–in–Publication Data

Williamson, Alicia, 1962–
  A seeking heart: rediscovering true worship/ Alicia Williamson, Sarah Groves.
     p. cm.
  ISBN 1-56309-737-0
  1. Worship. I. Groves, Sarah, 1965– II. Title.
  BV10.2 .G37 2000
  248.3—dc21 99-050718

Unless otherwise noted, all Scripture references are from the NEW AMERICAN STANDARD BIBLE, © Copyright The Lockman Foundation 1960, 1962, 1963, 1968, 1971, 1972, 1973, 1975, 1977. Used by permission.
or
From the Holy Bible, New International Version. Copyright © 1973, 1978, 1984, International Bible Society. Used by permission of Zondervan Bible Publishers.
Scripture quotations from *The Message*. Copyright © 1993, 1994, 1995. Used by permission.
Scripture quotations from the King James Version. Used by permission.

If you would like to have Alicia Williamson lead worship for your church, ministry, or organization, please contact Alicia Williamson c/o Capital Artist Agency, 277 Mallory Station Road, Franklin, TN 37064, (615) 771-6010.

If you would like to have Sarah Groves lead worship or speak for your church, ministry, or organization, please contact Sarah Groves, 816 Witt Street, Jonesboro, AR 72401, groves@alltel.net.

Cover design and illustration by Pam Moore of Steve Diggs and Friends Marketing/Communications

ISBN: 1-56309-737-0
N004107 • 0400 • 7.5M1

DEDICATION

From Alicia

 I dedicate this book to Kay Arthur and my friends associated with Precept Ministries. Of all the gifts I have ever received from family or friends, theirs is indeed the greatest. Thanks for the gift of instruction in learning *how* to study the word of God.

From Sarah

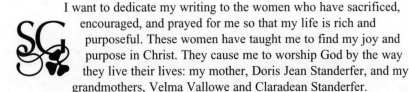 I want to dedicate my writing to the women who have sacrificed, encouraged, and prayed for me so that my life is rich and purposeful. These women have taught me to find my joy and purpose in Christ. They cause me to worship God by the way they live their lives: my mother, Doris Jean Standerfer, and my grandmothers, Velma Vallowe and Claradean Standerfer.

TABLE OF CONTENTS

❀ ❀ ❀

FOREWORD

I am sure that if you and I were able to sit and talk honestly you might agree, or even admit, there have been times in "worship" services when you have looked about and wondered if there was something wrong with you spiritually.

You find yourself in an ocean of hands moving as the waves of the sea gently caressing the shoreline, quietly retreating, and then returning for encore after encore as the same words are sung over and over and over again.

As you peer between the waves of hands, you see heads cast back in rapture and you wonder what is wrong with you. Eyes are closed. Lips move in unison praising the God of heaven, the Son, or the Spirit while bodies sway rhythmically to the music. Occasionally you catch a hand stopping the tears while others are permitted to stream unabated down the face and linger for a moment on the chin.

You're not crying. You are not deeply moved. You have no desire to raise your hands in "holy worship", to "just let go and yield to the Spirit" because personally you don't even "feel" the Spirit's presence even though the worship leaders have declared God is there in all His manifest power.

In fact you find yourself wearying of singing the same chorus over and over again—a chorus that has no depth of doctrine, a chorus that focuses on the worshiper rather than the One who is to be worshiped.

You are out of sync with the moment. You don't deny that others are moved, you don't deem their response not genuine, you are not their critic, their judge. The issue is not them, it's you. What is wrong with you?

Because something is not happening, does it mean, Beloved, that you are not a true worshiper of God, that you don't love God as those around you do? That is your question. Mine also.

If it means this, then I am not a worshiper of God for I have found myself in situations exactly like what I have described, and had I not known what the Word of God says, I would find myself condemned by my lack of emotion at the time.

Please don't get me wrong. Worship can be emotional—and believe me, I have felt the emotion to such a degree that I felt I had to fall to my knees or stand to my feet. Yet I have learned that although worship can be as I described, and be very real for some, it is not the only form worship takes. There is a depth to worship that goes far beyond the emotions to—at times—nothing but raw, determined, gut-level obedience when every emotion within you wants to turn and run rather than obey.

Alicia says it well: "Worship in its total essence is a response to truth." Although I have never had the privilege of working with Sarah, nor of meeting her, Alicia and I have ministered together on countless occasions in a variety of circumstances and situations. I have listened carefully to the words of her songs. We have studied and delighted in the Word together. She, too, studies God's Word inductively—the Word which sanctifies us because it is truth. Consequently I know when she leads us in "worship" through the avenue of music that the Word of God will never be sacrificed for the music—which, in my estimation, should always be the plumb line. When you study the history of revival, you will see that the effects of revival only endured and transformed men, women and children when the Word of God held the place of preeminence in the service. As Jesus said to the

Samaritan woman, those who worship God, must worship Him in spirit and truth.

It is my prayer that as a result of reading this book, of listening with your heart and mind to Sarah's illustrations and applications and Alicia's study of the Word on this subject of "A Seeking Heart, Rediscovering True Worship," you will find yourself poring over the Word of God. Lingering until it becomes your impetus to present yourself a living sacrifice (if you have not done so), holy and acceptable unto God, which is your reasonable service of worship. Not conformed to this world—nor man's interpretation of worship—but transformed by the renewing of your mind that you might rightly know and understand what the will of god is and do it as a true worshiper of the one and only True and Living God.

— *Kay Arthur*

A monogram at the beginning of each section
indicates which author is writing.

 Alicia Williamson

 Sarah Groves

ACKNOWLEDGEMENTS

From Alicia

 Thank you Elohim, our God and Creator, for placing in me the desire and ability to write about "The Missing Jewel"—worship! Thanks also for teaching me daily how to live in response to Your truth and not my circumstances. I love You.

Thanks to my darling husband, Richard, who never ceases to love me and encourage me to be all that God has created me to be. Thanks for your sacrifice in helping me "fulfill my ministry," which is now ours. I love you!

To Michael Chandler, who is just a few weeks from being born at the penning of this manuscript. The miracle of your life has made this mother a deeply grateful worshiper! I love you baby!

To Mom and Dad, my life-long encouragers! Thank you for living before me the life I have written about in this book, that of the True Worshiper. I love you!

From Sarah

 Thank you God for Your gifts and for the ability to dream, create, write, and communicate. Thank You for the privilege You give me to worship You and for the deep joy that is mine as I do.

Thanks to my husband, Mark, who has been my "first reader," my strong encourager, and a consistent loving support. Thank you for the many ways you help me to become all God created me to be. I love you.

Thanks to my dad, Ernest Standerfer, who has been a ready source of information, biblical knowledge, and inspiration. Thanks to my mom, Doris Jean Standerfer, who has spurred me on to be the best I can be and to write the best I can.

INTRODUCTION

Have you ever asked yourself why Christians are so divided on the issue of worship? I mean, do we raise our hands or not? Do we sing praise choruses or hymns? Do we stand or do we sit? Is it a church thing or an everyday thing? Is it a charismatic thing, or is the meaning of true worship left up to the individual for interpretation? The body of our precious Lord Jesus Christ is split over the subject of worship, yet worship should be the very thing that unites us.

Worship is everything I just mentioned and so much more. Worship in its total essence is a response to truth. Whether we are standing and shouting praise or reverently bowing as we experience the presence of God, every proper response to who God is, is an act of worship. When we write a tithe check, visit the poor and imprisoned, or welcome a new neighbor with a hot apple pie, we are worshiping God. We are responding to who He is and what He commands us to do. He is Master and Lord; therefore, to know Him and to obey Him is to truly worship Him.

Worship is much more than a song or a service. Worship is a lifestyle of service to God. Webster defines *worship* as "reverence offered to a divine being or supernatural power; also, an act of expressing such reverence." A biblical definition of *worship* is "to ascribe *worthship*." That simply means to give honor where honor is due. As children of God our responsibility is to live a life that is constantly ascribing worthship to God, in song and in service, day in and day out. The question that arises in my mind is how do we reverence something or someone we do not know? How do we ascribe worthship when we do not understand the worthiness of the one who is to receive our worship?

In Hosea 4:6 God said, "My people are destroyed for lack of knowledge. Because you have rejected knowledge, I also will reject you." Note here that God did not say that His people are going through a hard time because of a lack of knowledge, but that they are destroyed. I believe the core reason for our lack of passion for God is our lack of knowledge of God.

God is *perspicuous*. This simply means that God means to be understood. God expects us to know Him and obey Him. We know and obey God by knowing and obeying His word.

So what's the problem? You'll see many excuses we give for forsaking worship in this book. But the core problem is a lack of knowledge. Our busy lives have led us away from the word of God, and this absence of information is destroying our lives as true worshipers. Most of us have adopted the religion we grew up with, and have inherited a "style" of worship. I did. I was Baptist born and Baptist bred. I thought, "When I'm gone, I'll be a Baptist dead." How sad! God is not a Baptist. He is not Catholic. God is not Pentecostal. He's not even non-denominational. God is God. Just as the heavens are higher than the earth, so are His ways higher than our ways and His thoughts higher than our thoughts (Isa. 55:9).

Yet in our self-righteousness, we have created worship that is comfortable for us, whether God likes it or not. It's our thing. Some seem to have so much "new" revelation from God that His word is no longer enough. Others have become so sophisticated in their own thinking that God's word is beneath their intelligence. Tradition and religion have handed us a lie, or partial truth at best, and we have bought is as the will of God.

Enough is enough! Come! Sit with Sarah and me, in the presence of a Holy God, with this book, Bible, notepad, pen, and don't forget the hankie. Let's allow the Holy Spirit, our Resident Teacher, to teach us, from the word of God, what it biblically means to be a True Worshiper.

Chapter One

WORSHIP FROM KNOWING

AW I remember the day I had no words of worship to God. I had no song in my heart because my soul had been crushed with the terrible news that I had been diagnosed with cervical cancer. I went numb. I did not cry. I did not ask questions. I had no response whatsoever.

I drove myself home from the doctor's office. My husband, Richard, was there when I got in. I just looked at him with a dumb stare. There was truly nothing moving inside of me. At least that is the way I felt.

For days, I could not tell him about the appointment. I just let him think that it was a routine check-up and all was well. He had lost his mother to cervical cancer just a few years prior, and I just could not tell him that his new wife had been diagnosed with the same disease.

When I finally told him, his response was the same as mine. He said nothing and just stared at me. I knew that look and some of what he was feeling. First his mother and now his new bride. We had just celebrated our first anniversary.

God seemed to be nowhere. Everything seemed to stand still around us, except time. Time seemed to be running away from us as fast as it could, but we were too shocked to run after it. Life was horrible, and I blamed God for it.

After days had gone by and I had not uttered one word of praise or worship to God, I felt my soul truly dying. I had not heard from God and He had not heard from me. I guess anger,

hurt, and fear had damaged my emotions to the point of
deep depression.

One morning after Richard had gone to work, I made my
way to the living room couch. There, I uttered my first words to
God in days. "I'm not going to ask You to heal my body,
because if You say no, I am not ready for that answer. But I need
You to heal my soul. I need words from You, and whatever You
say is fine. Just heal my soul." That was the extent of my prayer.

Immediately, I heard His words in my soul. They were so
clear, I raised my head to look behind me. I thought someone
was in my home, or a radio or television was on. Nothing was on
and I was the only person there. Yet, I heard very clearly in my
soul what was being said to me, and I understood perfectly what
it meant. I immediately felt the strength of God. I asked Him to
"say it again." He did. He said it twice. "Healing comes from
knowing who I am."

I wrote it down on the first piece of paper I could find. That
sentence kept going through my mind. Every time I heard it, I
felt the strength of God. I kept meditating on it until I was strong
enough to hear all that He had to say to me that day.

The more I listened and meditated on His Word, the more
sure I was that I was hearing from God. That day, I believe Jesus
Christ opened the heavens and came and rescued my hurting soul
from the deepest depression I have ever known.

He just held me for a while, saying nothing, and that was
fine. I cried and He brushed away my tears. Then He washed my
soul with the healing water of His Word.

Knowing the Word

How well do you know the word of God? Are you daily
developing a personal relationship with Him through Scripture,
or are you perishing from a lack of knowledge?

I remember when I was perishing from a lack of knowledge. I had been in full-time ministry for less than a year, when I became very well aware of the fact that I had nothing new to say, and the old that I was saying was so old that it had become routine. I was hurting in my soul and was embarrassed to try and continue on in ministry. I wanted to quit and become an algebra teacher. I felt like I was dying.

I shared what I was going through with a dear friend, and she suggested that I go to a Bible study that was being held on Tuesday mornings. I readily agreed to go. I knew I needed water for my thirsty soul. We were going to study the book of Romans, for two years! Yea right. I thought I would be the smartest one in the class and just leave them all in the dust. It could not possibly take that long to study a letter that came in the mail.

Well, it did take two years. The book of Romans is the constitution of the Christian faith. I never realized that there was so much I did not know from the Bible. For two years, I struggled through my emotions. I was excited that I was learning so much. I was extremely frustrated when I did not understand. I bubbled over with joy when understanding came. My heart broke because I had missed so much for so long (and I grew up in church and in a Christian home). I wept for my lost friends and family. How would I ever get this good news to them? At the writing of this book, I am studying the book of Romans again! I just cannot get over the astounding truths that are there for the Christian faith.

Here is the question I really want you to answer. In reference to the Bible, do you ask yourself and others, "What do you think that means?" If this is your only approach to God's word, you will never know God.

Remember, worship is a response to truth, not a response to what we as individuals think that truth is. If you and others, maybe even your Sunday School class or Bible study group, are still trying to decide for yourselves what you think God's word means, then you are probably leaving your study times with fifteen or twenty different opinions about any given passage.

Psalm 119:160 says, "The sum of Thy word is truth, and every one of Thy righteous ordinances is everlasting." Oh, how we need to understand the whole counsel of God's word and to live lives that are constantly responding to it. In 2 Timothy 2:15 Paul wrote to Timothy, "Study to shew thyself approved unto God, a workman that needeth not to be ashamed, rightly dividing the word of truth" (KJV). The word study here comes from the Greek word *spoudazo*, meaning to hasten, or to exert oneself, to put forth effort, to be diligent. The NASB translation says, "Be diligent to present yourself approved to God as a workman who does not need to be ashamed, handling accurately the word of truth."

God has scolded us for our lack of knowledge and has commanded us to be diligent students of the word. Why? Because He means to be understood.

What a great verse! Study and be diligent because the person whose approval you want to meet is God. Remember the sum of His word is truth. When we choose to respond to His truth, we are living a lifestyle of true worship.

I have found that when I take this attitude toward the Bible—that is to diligently study it and know God through His word—I am able to answer three very important questions that help me clearly understand what God is saying.

The questions are:

1. *What does God's word say?*
2. *What does God's word mean?*
3. *How do I apply what it says and what it means to my life?*

You may recognize this as the Inductive Method of studying the Bible. You are right. I have found that the most effective way to know God through His Word is by observing what His Word says. That is called *observation*. Secondly, by allowing Scripture to interpret Scripture, I am able to determine what a passage means. That is called *interpretation*. Note that I have not *yet* gone to a commentary or book about the Bible. Thirdly, after I know what a passage says, and after I know what the Bible says about that particular passage, then and only then am I able to apply what it says and what it means to my life. That is called *application*.

Observation, interpretation, and application lead to a great transformation. This is God's purpose in sending us His word. He expects us to know what His Word says and means, and then allow this transforming truth to cause us to live differently. After we have carefully observed the text and have cross-referenced it, we can go to commentaries and other resources that may bring us deeper understanding.

God's word will either change our lives or it will leave us without excuse. The life that constantly responds to God is the life lived in true worship! Second Peter 1:3 says that God's divine power has granted to us everything pertaining to life and godliness, through the true knowledge of Him.

As New Testament believers, we have such a tremendous advantage in gaining knowledge about our God. We have the Bible, which is the inspired word of God, and we have the Holy Spirit, our resident teacher, teaching us all that God's word says and means and showing us how to apply it to everyday life.

Second Peter 1:4–7 goes on to say, "For by these He has grant-ed to us His precious and magnificent promises, in order that by them you might become partakers of *the* divine nature, having escaped the corruption that is in the world by lust. Now for this very reason also, applying all diligence, in your faith supply moral excellence, and in *your* moral excellence, knowledge; and in *your* knowledge, self-control, and in *your* self-control, perseverance, and in *your* perseverance, godliness; and in *your* godliness, brotherly kindness, and in *your* brotherly kindness, love."

Now, it's obvious that these things will take some time and effort on our part. This process will take our developing a relationship with God through Scripture, as well as our allowing His Holy Spirit to guide us into all truth. Look at what we will gain through the "true knowledge" of God.

"For if these *qualities* are yours and are increasing, they render you neither useless nor unfruitful in the true knowledge of our Lord Jesus Christ" (2 Peter 1:8). When we possess a true knowledge of Jesus Christ, and are increasing in that knowledge and in that relationship, we become useful and fruitful. Now this is the lifestyle of a true worshiper.

We live in response to God and not in response to our circumstances. I have found that the things we make a big issue over (like the simple gesture of raising hands in a worship service) become a non-issue. When we see God as Abba, that gesture makes all the sense in the world. Every child will come to a loving Papa with arms wide open, full of love and trust.

When We Don't Know Him

I have found that the more knowledge I gain of who God is, the more I do indeed love and trust Him. Knowledge, love, and trust work simultaneously in our lives as true worshipers. Sarah will discuss this in an upcoming chapter. However, knowing the word of God is the beginning to true worship.

Consider the other side of this coin. "For he who lacks these *qualities* is blind *or* short-sighted, having forgotten *his* purification from his former sins" (2 Peter 1:9).

Are you blinded by sin or shortsighted by religion? Have you been washed clean of a guilty conscience by the water of the word of God?

"Therefore, brethren, be all the more diligent to make certain about His calling and choosing you; for as long as you practice these things, you will never stumble" (2 Peter 1:10).

Not only are we reminded to be diligent, but to be all the more diligent, and ever increasing in knowledge, so that we do not stumble into a lifestyle that is not pleasing to the Lord.

"For in this way the entrance into the eternal kingdom of our Lord and Savior Jesus Christ will be abundantly supplied to you" (2 Peter 1:11).

The kingdom of God awaits you. What an inheritance! Let's not stumble around in the darkness of ignorance and unbelief, but let us turn on the light of God's truth and live this wonderful life of true worship. Knowing and obeying God's word is the only way we will know true victory in our lives. It is the only way we will develop a lifestyle of true worship.

Are you willing to experience healing from knowing God? Are you ready to allow the Holy Spirit to teach you God's word? You may first need to deal with things in your life that have distracted you from God. Sarah will help you identify these in the next chapter. But if you are willing, then your worship, which is your response to God's truth, will be with joy unspeakable and full of glory. When I had no words of worship, God gave me *His* word. ✂

Healing

I don't want to be your last resort.
I want to be your very first choice.
I Am able to meet your needs.
Child I can see your feeble body.
I can even feel your pain
And your healing lies in
The power of My name.
I Am able to heal the sick
Able to raise the dead
I am the Lord Jehovah
The Truth, the Life, the Way
I Am the Sovereign Lord of All
And I hold you in My hands
Healing comes from KNOWING
Who I Am.
I want to heal your broken spirit
I want to heal your broken dreams
I am willing
To ease your pain
Not one thing happens in your life
Before it passes through My hands
I control all things
So you can trust my plan.
Your prayers don't always work out
The way you think they should
But I've promised to work all things
Together for your good.
I Am able to heal the sick
Able to raise the dead
I Am the Lord Jehovah
The Truth, the Life, the Way
I Am the Sovereign Lord of All
And I hold you in My hands.
Healing comes from knowing
Healing comes from knowing
Healing comes from knowing

"Healing"
(Alicia Williamson) From *Faithful Heart*
© 1998 Alicia-Renee Publishing, ADM by CMI (Nashville, TN).
Mobile, Alabama

Chapter Two

LOSING SIGHT OF
TRUE WORSHIP

Have you experienced a spiritual high, only to fall to the depths of your relationship with God when it was over? What knocked you off your mountaintop experience? I was on a spiritual high one summer in college. I dedicated that summer to mission work in New York. I grew spiritually, developed close friend-ships, and experienced God using and strengthening my gifts in ministry. I knew the joy of being in God's will. I returned to my college campus and felt I could take on the world. I believed literally the Scripture that Paul declared, "I have become all things to all men that by all means I might save some" (1 Cor. 9:22). I was already involved in many activities and I flung myself into more, believing that I could be a witness to all kinds of people through various organizations and activities. (And I did have to study a little bit in there somewhere!)

For a while, I was extremely busy, but loving every minute of it. Then it happened. To use a popular phrase, "I crashed and burned." I went from one of the highest points of my life to one of the lowest. I faced burnout.

I had to acknowledge the fact that I could not do and be everything to everyone, no matter how well intentioned my heart was. I became depressed and discouraged. My *feelings* of being close to God were the first to go. By faith, I chose to continue believing God was there with me, but I felt alone and that God was far away. My despair didn't go away overnight, though I prayed it would. My depression didn't lift miraculously, though I desired it to. But over time, I learned more about God and myself

and gained some handles for life that have helped me since—
another gift of His amazing grace!

I am now years from that experience, but I know that trusting
in God and worshiping Him was and is key to how we approach
both the painful and joyous occurrences in our life. The despair and
depression did lift, but it was a daily, gradual process as I trusted
in God even though I could not see or feel Him. I worshiped God
and read His promises back to Him. Worship, prayer, and faith
brought me to a place where I could celebrate who God was and
who I was in Christ.

In my adult life, I still face the challenge of taking on too
many activities, feeling I can help other people if I do this and
that. (I am the person that everybody loves when they need a job
to get done!) The challenge is especially true as it relates to my
personal worship of God.

I can allow busyness with work, family, church, and ministry
to become more dominant than my personal communion with
God. Worship becomes a low priority, not intentionally, but easily, and other things start taking priority in the hectic pace of life.

In one way or another, we all have a seeking heart. Our hearts
yearn for God's touch, even when we don't realize it. Our lives
get dry and need to be filled with God's wellspring of love. When
we worship God, we are changed, transformed. We become more
like Christ and more aligned to God's desires for our lives. Our
seeking hearts find their homes in God and we are made whole,
changed by His presence in our lives.

Women of Worship

I remember a particular worship experience with women of
different backgrounds lifting their hearts and lives to God. Most
of the women at the event had little in common, and yet they were
bound together by their Christian faith and their true worship.

As the group lifted their voices in praise singing "Amazing Grace," each seemed to have a great understanding of God's goodness and grace. Three females, in particular, caught my attention and taught me more about what it means to be a true worshiper.

Jane, a woman well-acquainted with city street-life, had been homeless. She had become a Christian and was working to rebuild her life with God's help. I could not ignore the sincerity in her worship. Jane truly understood what it meant to be lost and then found—she had experienced God's grace. Her response to that truth was worship, praise, and love for God.

Laura, a successful businesswoman and single mother of one, also lifted her voice in worship. As I watched Laura, I knew her worship was authentic because she too understood her dependence on God's grace for her daily life. Having become a Christian as a young adult, she was still growing in understanding of what it meant to follow Christ. She desired to give her busy life to the Lord. She wanted Him to be glorified through her, as she, too, was a recipient of God's amazing grace.

Another female in the room, Megan, was about nine years old. She had purity, unquestioning faith in God, and honesty in her worship. God's amazing grace was evident as He was a part of this young girl's life at an early age. Even Megan had been spiritually blind before she met Christ, but now saw and understood that she had a Savior and Lord in Jesus Christ. Her purity of heart and simple, childlike faith challenged me to come before God in the same way.

What about you and your worship? Has God's love and amazing grace changed your life? Is your love for God expressed in true worship? When we experience God's amazing grace, we can't help but worship Him. Our love for God propels us to express that love in worship.

In my life, I have encountered Christian women with hearts full of God-given desire to truly worship Him with all they are. They have experienced God's grace and are actively growing in a personal relationship with Him. These women love to worship God and have learned how to live a lifestyle of worship.

I see other Christian women who desire to have growing relationships with God and to worship Him meaningfully, yet they face obstacles in their lives that hinder their relationships with God and thus, their worship of Him. And other women are lost, searching, and seeking something better in their lives. They are looking for meaning and purpose, and yet they have not come to believe or understand that meaning and purpose are found in God's love and grace. They need a relationship with Him.

God created both male and female, living human beings, because He wanted to have fellowship with us. God shaped us so that at the very core of who we are, we have a longing—a yearning—to know and worship God and to find our purpose in Him.

Helen Keller lived her life blind and deaf. As an eight-year-old, she asked questions like, "Where did I come from? Where shall I go when I die?" No one had ever communicated to her about God up to that time. According to her biography, most likely no one had ever attempted to do so. Without the opportunity to see God's creation or hear Scripture and prayers, without much communication at all with others, Helen Keller had a yearning to understand why she was here, what her purpose was, and where she would be for eternity. Though she didn't understand it, she had a longing for God and for fellowship with Him.

No matter our life circumstances, our economic or social status, our nationality or heart language, God created us to know Him and to enjoy Him forever. As His precious children, He enjoys us and takes great delight in us. God finds pleasure when His cherished creations come to Him in worship and fellowship.

Where are You?

Today women are busier than ever. Many have full-time jobs and/or full-time families. They are often distracted by hectic activities, family concerns, and demanding careers. Some women are looking for change, bored with their life routine. Other women don't have time to even think about change, while some are devoted Christians and have been for many years. Others are brand-new Christians with a passion to love, understand, and worship God. Others are lost, without hope or truth, and are searching for answers.

The fact that you are reading this book indicates that you want to gain a better understanding of worship. You are taking the first step to rediscover true worship. If you feel you have lost sight of true worship, I hope this book will be an instrument that God uses to guide your seeking heart into the joy of His presence.

In the process of writing this book, I surveyed women of varying ages from a variety of Christian denominations. This chapter, in particular, reveals some of the results of that survey. Their stories will give a broad overview of topics that Alicia and I will deal with more in-depth later in the book. I appreciate those women who shared, in many cases very candidly, about their struggles to know and worship God. Perhaps you will identify with their life situations and struggles, as well as my own, and will be challenged and equipped to be a true worshiper of God.

What's Worship?

Some of us have limited worship to one hour on Sunday mornings. Sadly, that is the extent of worship for many people. Most of us know worship is more, but we may get bogged down thinking that worship has to be done in a certain format or a certain way for God to be pleased. We think we have to go through certain steps, play one kind of music, or be in a certain geographical place to get "into His presence."

There is so much more! Throughout His word, God expresses His desire for a relationship with you in which you know and love Him. As you seek to know God more and spend time getting to know Him, you will discover the power and joy that comes only from Him and that He gives us as we worship and follow Him.

Anne Ortlund, noted author of *Up With Worship* and a pastor's wife, says "Naturally, when Christians come together, they meet not God, but each other." She also says, "Many Christians spend their lives in horizontal activities such as Sunday School classes, women's meetings or gatherings, home Bible studies, even church services. They learn to know *about* God, but often never learn to *know* God." Many Christians seem to use church services as a time to talk a little about Him, but mostly as an excuse to see each other.

It is most important to connect with God! Be careful not to mistake talking about Him or being around people who do as truly connecting with Him. Knowing God personally, meeting with Him, is vital for our lives. As we know Him, our response is worship, adoration, praise, and thanksgiving.

Worship involves giving ourselves completely to the lordship of Christ. Talmage Williams, author of *The Worshipgiver*, says, "Worshiping God is more than participating in worship activities, worship services, and worship experiences; it is the recognition and affirmation with our whole being that God really is sovereign God. Genuine worship of the true God involves the submitting of our minds, bodies, emotions, and spirits to God's sovereign lordship. Our faith in God expresses itself in awe, adoration, and praise to the Eternal God who has revealed Himself in Jesus Christ."

Worship encompasses much more than showing up for church services. However, *corporate worship* is important for the Christian life. Hebrews 10:25 reminds us not to forsake our assembling together as Christian believers. *Personal worship*, time spent alone with God in recognizing and affirming who God is, is also vital for your Christian life. As we are actively engaged in both of these worship experiences, we are able to develop a *lifestyle of worship*.

When we develop a lifestyle of worship, we learn that our jobs, families, personal lives, hobbies, church involvement, and ministries can all be expressions of worship of the One who knows us best and loves us completely. We need to experience meaningful, personal, and corporate worship as Christian believers. Yet, all of our lives can be an expression of worship.

Colossians 3:17 reads, "And whatever you do, whether in word or deed, do it all in the name of the Lord Jesus, giving thanks to God the Father through him." *The Message* paraphrase expresses Colossians 3:17 in this way, "Let every detail in your lives— words, actions, whatever—be done in the name of the Master, Jesus, thanking God every step of the way." God promises to never leave us alone. Since He is always with us, shouldn't everything we do, say, think, and live be worship to God? We hope to challenge you in this book to develop a lifestyle that honors God in all you are, do, say, and think. We call this a lifestyle of worship.

I'm Just Too Busy

Susan has a full-time job, is an active member of her church, and loves to decorate her home and yard. Laura is a married mother of two, a member of the church choir, a Sunday School teacher, and can't remember a time when she had a moment for herself. Beth is a busy, full-time student and holds a part-time job. She is a leader in her church's college ministry.

If you knew these women personally, you might call them dynamic Christian women. While God is using them in great ways, each of them shares a yearning to slow down and experience God.

Well aware of Psalm 46:10, they know it is important to "be still and know that He is God," yet they struggle to take time to be with God. Moving at a fast pace through life, each feels that her greatest barrier to worshiping God actively, consistently, and meaningfully is busyness. Their active lives keep them from having time to spend with God.

In my survey, I found busyness to be the most common obstacle that keeps women from worshiping God. Christian women truly want to worship God, but find it hard to make time to do so. This is not a surprise really. Women are more active and have more opportunities now than at any other time in history. We have more options than we sometimes know what to do with. Well-meaning Christian women can be busy with so much, including Christian work and service, that in the midst of the busyness a freshness of the Spirit is lost and our relationship with God is stifled. Fulfilling responsibilities and duties becomes more necessary to us than spending time in personal devotion and worship. Author and speaker Esther Burroughs has it right when she says in her book *Empowered*, "Busyness is one of the greatest deterrents to the Spirit of God working in the lives of Christians today."

What about you? Is busyness a barrier in your own personal, spiritual life? I resonate with the women I have mentioned, for I too find the number one barrier to worshiping God is often busyness. God understands our busy lives, yet it is important that we take a deep look into our lives to see if we are pleasing Him. He knows the schedule we keep, the pace at which we live each day, and the very intricate details of each one of us. He lavishes His grace on us, and He also longs to be the most important part of our lives.

I mentioned in the introduction my challenge with busyness and activity. I have the personality type that likes to be doing things, staying active and on the move. I like variety and diversity. I like all sorts of people and most of the time, I even like change.

Allowing my activities to become more prominent than worship is always a struggle for me. Recently, I resigned from my full-time ministry job and am now working out of my home. My husband, Mark, and I moved to a new city and state. We have been submerged in change, as occurs with any relocation. Amidst busy changes, the challenge to make personal worship of God a priority isn't an easy task.

When I was working full-time as National Youth Consultant for Woman's Missionary Union, I would often wake up in the morning (and sometimes throughout the night) thinking of all the many things I needed to do and wanted to accomplish. I loved my job, but I often struggled to make time for personal worship. Even in full-time Christian ministry, I found it hard to nurture a life-style of worship. I had trouble blocking out distractions so that I could focus on the Lord.

I wish I could tell you I found the secret key or answer to this dilemma, but what I can tell you is that it takes a daily choice to spend time with God and to live our lives in worship. You are the only person that can make this choice for yourself. God will guide you and help you, but you have to make the decision to not miss or replace the time you spend in personal worship and devotion with other things. When we don't, our busyness becomes a sin in our lives. There is just no way around it.

We have to make a firm, committed choice to say we will take the time for God. Proverbs 4:23 says, "Watch over your heart with all diligence, for from it flows the springs of life." I know it isn't easy, but I am steadfastly convinced that it is worth the effort. To know and experience God and His presence in your life, to worship Him and experience a meaningful relationship with Him, is worth the time.

Jesus was extremely busy. There were great demands on His life. But He was always able to distinguish the important from the urgent. He was consistently finding a quiet place, away from others, to be with God, to pray, and to stay close to His Father. He is certainly our greatest role model for living.

Being sensitive to God's Spirit is hard when we are running fast, often on empty. As you examine your life, you may find that busyness has become sin in your life—sin "that so easily entangles us" declares the writer of Hebrews.

Busyness usually doesn't really feel like sin. After all, serving God can keep us very busy doing great things. If our busy lives become a personal barrier between us and the One who desires to be the Lord of our lives, then it is important to confess that sin and make right our relationship with Him. And sometimes we choose to busy ourselves with activity rather than deal with a deeper issue in our lives. It could be "hidden sins" that we hope others never notice and we try to rationalize away. We increase our activity rather than take time to be still and honest with God. Alicia shared a quote with me recently, "If the devil can't make us bad, he'll make us busy."

You may be saying, "Yes, okay, I understand that busyness can be a sin, but I don't see any way out of this busy life that has become such a constant for me." I believe that as we submit our entire life to our Lord, in His grace, He will show us what we are to do so that we can *live* as He wants us to and *be* who He created us to be. Only God can reveal that to you, and it is important to respond to Him in obedience if you want Him to truly be the Lord of your life. For some women, looking honestly at their lives before the Lord may result in taking a break or sabbatical from a job or duty. For another, it may be simply rearranging her schedule so that she gives priority to her time with God. Whatever it is for you, know that God wants the best for you and He wants you to draw closer to Him. James 4:8 says "Come near to God and He will come near to you." God wants all of us, not parts, not the leftovers—all of me and all of you. As we submit our lives, our schedules, and our activities to the Lord, He will be faithful to show us His desire for our lives. God's way is, and always will be, best.

I'm Distracted

As you read this book, you may be carrying a heavy load of personal problems, family crisis, loss, grief, and other burdens. These issues or circumstances can often distract and even consume us. God understands that. It is important, no matter what you are facing, to turn to Him, to trust Him, and to know God doesn't leave you alone.

A wonderful Christian woman in her late fifties shared with me of the deep pain she suffered when she lost her husband of many years to cancer. She told me that what helped her most was continuing to be in the corporate worship service of her church every Sunday and doing her best to worship. Sometimes she could hardly mutter a prayer or sing a song, but God used the experience of corporate worship to sustain her through her grief and to bring about healing in her life. Worshiping with other Christian believers, her church family, helped to bring her the comfort and strength she needed. In her grief, she didn't lose sight of the importance of worship. The time of corporate worship helped her to turn her focus on God—to reach out to Him and to worship Him, rather than just on her own grief.

In June 1998, I hung up the phone after talking with one of my grandmothers. I expressed my thanks to God for giving me the blessing of grandparents who have lived full and long lives. Having never lost anyone who was very close to me to death, particularly family members, I began to pray a prayer, "Lord, prepare me for loss. I don't know how I will handle it when I lose someone close to me. I know my grandparents are getting

older. I don't know if I will be able to handle their deaths.
Prepare me for loss. Prepare me so that when that time comes, I
will be able to handle it with You."

Less than a week later, I went on a business trip to Salt Lake
City, Utah, accompanied by my husband, Mark. I was three
months pregnant and we were just beginning to share our joyous
news with family and friends. The day after we arrived, we
found ourselves in a hospital in Salt Lake City going through a
miscarriage. It was a time of great loss for us.

Our feelings were mostly sadness, vulnerability, and shock,
but after we returned to our home in Birmingham, Alabama, I
remembered that prayer I had prayed. Could God have been so
intimately acquainted with me, that as His Spirit put that prayer
on my heart and lips, He was preparing me for what we were
about to go through? It is hard for me to put into words the level
of intimacy and depth of God's presence that I felt during this
time, but it was very real and deep.

Because the experience is so personal, sharing it with you
isn't easy for me. Mark and I had a choice to blame God or to
blame other things, but over time as the grief has become less
intense, we've recognized that God is faithful, that to not worship Him means we miss out. God does sustain us, comfort us,
and guide us through the overwhelming experiences of life. To
choose not to live our lives in worship of Him dismisses the
blessings that we experience and that come, even through crisis,
pain, and loss.

God is so far beyond our comprehension that words sometimes fail to express the power and depth of who God is to us. In
our most difficult times, we are able to know God in a way that
we would never have known Him if we hadn't had that experience. Don't miss out on what God wants you to know about Him
and yourself because you are distracted. Keep worshiping and

trusting Him. God will bless you as you continue to seek and serve Him.

God understands what we go through more than we understand. Jeremiah 29:11 reminds us that God gives us a future and a hope and that we can put our trust in Him, even when He may seem far away. "For I know the plans I have for you, declares the Lord, plans to prosper you and not to harm you, plans to give you hope and a future." If you are filled with distractions, seek and ask for God's help. Put your trust in Him daily. Continue to express your worship to Him and allow God to become your focus.

I'm Not Good Enough

Tammy is a young woman in her twenties who is serving the Lord. When she was a child, she was the victim of family physical abuse. She blamed herself for the abuse and for her adopted parents' divorce. For a lot of reasons, she felt unlovable and contemplated suicide as a teenager. Tammy met the Lord as a high school student and God has been working in her life ever since. For most of her life, she thought no one could love her, especially God. She thought she wasn't good enough.

You may think that you have to be a perfect person in order for God to love you and accept you. Even as a Christian, you may think that in order to worship God, you have to be sinless or perfect. When we read Scripture and look at the life of Jesus, we see how He never demanded that people "get it all together" before a relationship with Him could occur. He sought out those who were greedy, active adulterers, destitute, those filled with pride, bar frequenters, and criminals. He never said or indicated that you had to become perfect before He would be a part of your life. God loves us and accepts us so much that He sent His Son just for us.

Some women are carrying around baggage that has become a
barrier to their spiritual growth and ability to worship God. They
compare themselves to others, thinking that they just don't measure up to other Christians. A common remark is, "They seem
perfect and I am quite aware that I am not." Psalm 139:14 says,
"I praise you because I am fearfully and wonderfully made; your
works are wonderful, I know that full well."

We are fearfully and wonderfully made, and God's works are
wonderful. You, therefore, are a wonderful work of God!
Because God created us, He knows us and fully understands that
we fail and we mess up. We need His grace and our loving God
wants to give that mercy to us. He wants us to live our lives for
Him, but He doesn't leave us alone to do that. He loves us, wants
the best for us, and wants to help us to be all He created us to be.
No matter who you are, where you've been, or what you've done,
God loves you and delights in the worship you offer to Him out
of an honest and sincere heart. That is good news!

I Don't Know Enough About the Bible

Have you ever played a game where you were blindfolded
and led around obstacles by someone else? You knew you were
not getting the full picture because you were wearing the blind-
fold. This reason for not worshiping is a good one because it is
impossible to respond appropriately to someone or something we
don't know. Just as Alicia emphasized in the previous chapter,
the same is true of God and our worship of Him. John 4:23–24
says "Yet a time is coming and has now come when the true
worshipers will worship the Father in spirit and truth, for they
are the kind of worshipers the Father seeks. God is spirit and His
worshipers must worship in spirit and truth."

In order to be true worshipers, we must seek to know God.
To know Him involves spending time with Him through Bible

study and prayer. As we study God's word, we come to understand that our purpose for living is to be in fellowship with God—to love and worship Him. The Bible is our guidebook to understand our purpose for life, as well as to know more about our God who desires our worship.

In Mark 12:28–34 a religious teacher asked Jesus what was the greatest commandment. Jesus declared, "Love the Lord God with all your heart and with all your soul and with all your mind and with all your strength." The most important thing required to develop a life of worship is to allow Christ to be the Lord and Savior of your life. Without accepting Him and His love for you, you will have trouble finding the real joy and peace He gives as you grow in a relationship with Him. The relationship begins as we understand God's love for us and that Jesus Christ wants to be the most important thing in our lives.

Carrying out the greatest commandment Jesus gave will give us an increased understanding of who God is. We will grow in our ability to love God and to express our love to Him through worship. As we learn to love God with all our heart, soul, mind, and strength, we will become the true worshipers that He desires His beloved followers to be.

I'm Bored

Since women are busier than ever these days, I was baffled to discover that a barrier to worship is boredom. What I have learned from women who give boredom as a reason for the lack of worship in their lives is that they usually don't know how to worship. Also, boredom is often an indication that their personal relationship with God has grown stale. Perhaps life circumstances have contributed. These women may feel they are in a boring routine of life they don't see changing anytime soon. Established traditions may lead to boring worship experiences.

Every church that has been in existence, even for a short time, has traditions. Some of these are beneficial and help to unify members. We often like the traditions of the church. They help us know what to expect. If there ever comes a time where traditions of the church become more important than worshiping God in spirit and truth, we fail as Christian believers in our obedience to live, serve, and worship. When tradition takes the place of true worship, the power of God is weakened and diminished.

Tradition can also become a barrier to worship in our personal lives, causing us to feel bored. We may have a devotional time set to offer our worship to God each day, but we stick to the same routine to the point that our connection with God is momentary at best. We pray, without really allowing God's Spirit to move in us, direct us, or speak to us. We go through motions because it is more convenient or less time-consuming. Perhaps tradition has weakened, rather than strengthened, your worship of God. Be aware and sensitive that following established tradition is easier than seeking God and His Word.

True worship comes from an open, sincere heart. If you have grown bored and stale in your relationship with God, then true worship probably isn't happening. Check your heart and see if you have lost the freshness of your love for God. We all get into ruts at times, but let me encourage you to go before God and come to Him again. Just as the father of the prodigal son welcomed him home with open arms and a celebration, so God will do for you. He loves you that much.

I'm Lazy

When some women think of worship, they think of a boring religious exercise lacking spiritual power and authenticity. Sadly, some church worship services fit this description. While church worship services may or may not enhance our worship, personal worship of God is not *dependent* on anything external. Your corporate worship services may have become routine for you, but if you are growing as a Christian believer, you can worship God *independent* of what is going on outside of you. This can happen in both personal and corporate worship.

Laziness is another reason women stated as an obstacle to worship. I appreciate the honesty of women that said, "I want to worship. I desire to experience God in true worship, but I am often too lazy to make the effort." One woman declared her need for accountability and asked for help.

Women, we need each other. Our uniqueness as women provides us the ability to encourage and inspire each other. We need fellow Christian women who can hold us accountable, who will remind us of the importance of nurturing our relationship with God, and help us in our pursuit of God.

Think of one person who helps you to grow in your relationship with God. Thank God for the gift of that person in your life. Now think of one person you can encourage to nurture her or his spiritual life with God. Pray for that person, and look for ways you can be an encourager.

I'm Afraid

Fear is another barrier stated by women who want to worship God. They sincerely express some anxiety about being completely open and honest with God in worship. It might be that they have had religious experiences called worship where they felt manipulated by worship leaders or forced to do or express something that they were not comfortable with. It could be they have been exposed to worship styles or experiences where they felt uncomfortable.

God has made each of us unique, with special personalities, learning styles, interests, and relationships. Creator God knows you and wants you to know Him. God is pleased with every expression of worship you offer when it is done with sincerity out of love and reverence for God. There is not a prescribed act of worship that is better or more spiritual than any other. God loves you and delights in your unique worship of Him. God's Spirit is with you when you worship and you can respond to His Spirit in truth. Second Timothy 1:7 says, "For God did not give us a spirit of timidity, but a spirit of power, of love and of self-discipline."

All of Me

A college student who is preparing for a career in ministry spoke recently in my church on the topic of worship. Steve challenged our church with a great analogy. He said, "Worship is a celebration of who God is." In many celebrations or parties in our lives, we send invitations inviting people we care about. We write *RSVP* at the bottom of the invitation sending the message that the person or persons invited are to let us know if they will attend. Usually celebrations and parties are just what their name describes. Anticipation, excitement, and joy often accompany these events. Steve asked the church, "What is your RSVP to God as He invites you to worship Him?"

And so, I ask you the same question. Will your response to God be, "I'm just too busy" or "I am too bored and lazy to come to Your celebration." Will you say, "Going to a party is not a part of what I normally do, so I should decline"? Or, "I don't have all my life together yet, so I better not come." How would you feel if you heard these responses from friends you invited? Our relationship with God and our worship of Him can be very similar. God invites us to worship and celebrate all of who He is. Because He knows what is best for us, He is disappointed with excuses that keep us from worshiping Him. How will you respond to God's invitation?

For us to truly worship God, we must be willing to come to God with all that we are. As we give ourselves to Him, we truly worship God.

As we make specific efforts to spend focused time worshiping Him, our lives are changed. We are transformed by God for His good purposes and plans for our lives. When we give ourselves completely to Him, we can experience an intimate relationship with God, the fullness of His love, and the abundant life God wants to give each of us. Alicia and I wrote a worship chorus that is a prayer from our hearts. May this be your prayer as we all become true worshipers with faithful hearts. ⚘

Change Me
From The Inside Out

Change me from the inside out
and I will sing Your praise.

Change me from the inside out
and I'll follow You all my days.

Everything I am, All I hope to be,

Every dream I dream, I give you all of me

Change me from the inside out
and they'll see Christ in me.

Chapter Three

PASSIONATE PURSUIT

He had gorgeous blue eyes, flowing blond hair, and a winning smile. I became captivated with this fellow one summer day. Basking in the sun by the swimming pool, attempting to catch a nap, I was awakened by loud yells of "marco polo" by a group of teenagers in the pool. As my eyes were drawn to the activity in the pool, I noticed the young boy riding along in his animal float as his mother pushed him slowly around the pool. (Not what you were expecting, huh?) My guess is that he was about two years old.

Drawn in by his content and joyous smile, I began to think what a great example he was when it comes to experiencing the contentment that comes from trusting and resting in God. It brings peace and deep joy to our lives. As we love God and because we love God, we have deep delight in Him. This little boy was a great example of this true and sheer delight.

Psalm 37:4 says, "Delight yourself in the Lord, and he will give you the desires of your heart." When I hear people quote this verse or refer to it, usually the focus is on the last half of the sentence. "He will give you the desires of your heart." After all, we hope and want to believe that our deepest dreams and desires will become reality. We long to have what we want. Do you hear that? Have what we want.

We miss the whole point of this verse and this Psalm when we move past the first part of the verse quickly without letting it sink in and letting the Holy Spirit show us His truth. When we fail to act on what it says, we miss the point of the verse. It is the "Delight yourself in the Lord" part. The verb tense of the word *delight* means "to take great pleasure, to give keen enjoyment, or to give joy or satisfaction to." The noun tense means "joy, extreme satisfaction, a high degree of gratification."

Developing a lifestyle of worship begins with developing a love relationship with God where we delight in God. We take pleasure in just being with Him and giving our love, affection, and attention to Him.

That summer day, I saw a wonderful picture of delight. This child was so content with his circumstances because he knew and loved the one who was guiding and protecting him. When we are in a trusting relationship with the Father, we can rest continually, not just momentarily, in Him. We can know He is right there with us guiding, protecting, and caring for us. This is a joyous truth.

Amidst the noise, the little boy seemed undaunted, and his mother was, as well. They were content to just be together, to peacefully swim around despite all the swirls and screams around them. The smile never left the boy's face and the mother, careful to care for and protect her son, was enjoying the moment perhaps just as completely.

At moments the boy would reach to and hold his mother's hand, not out of fear, but out of love. He seemed delighted to be with her in that moment. How like our relationship with God. He is faithful to guide us through the crazy world we live in and He enjoys us. When we are able to delight in Him, in His presence, we bring God pleasure. Psalm 16:11 says, "In thy presence is fullness of joy, in thy right hand are pleasures evermore." He desires for us to experience a fullness of joy that comes from knowing Him and His presence. This fullness of joy surpasses any joy that the world or any other relationship offers.

When we are too busy to be "in the moment," worried or distracted with the past or future, we miss the fullness of joy that God offers us and wants us to experience.

Mind and Heart

Developing a lifestyle of worship involves a wholehearted, passionate pursuit of God. Intentionally seeking God through prayer, desiring to know Him, communing with Him, focusing on His Word, and serving Him daily develop in us a lifestyle of worship and enable us to be true worshipers.

But before we come to God, He pursues a love relationship with us. He desires for us to be in a loving relationship with Him. As we pursue a relationship with Him (just as He pursues us), we can't help but worship.

I learned a definition of worship from one of my seminary professors, Dr. Bruce Leafblad. "Worship involves setting our mind's attention and heart's affection on God." I like this definition because it helps us understand that our role must be intentional. Setting our mind's attention on God—deliberately putting our minds, our thoughts, our intellect on God and who He is—is vital for worship. Worship will not happen without involvement or action on our part. Setting our mind's attention on God includes knowing who God is, learning more about who He is, and choosing to focus our attention on Him.

To set our heart's affection on God means to direct our love, devotion, passion, desire, and commitment on or to God. Colossians 3:2 says, "Set your affections on things above, not on things on the earth" (KJV). What or who is the primary target of your affection? Many of us might say our families and others we love. God wants us to love our families as He loves us. He is glorified through Christian living and Christian families. However, He also understood that the people we love deeply and dearly can become a hindrance to following Christ when they become more important than He is. In Matthew 10:37–39, Jesus said, "Anyone who loves his father and mother more than me is not worthy of me; anyone who loves his son or daughter more than me is not worthy of me; and anyone who does not take his cross and follow me is not worthy of me. Whoever finds his life will lose it, and whoever loses his life for my sake will find it."

Some of us might not say it, but in truth we know that we allow material things to become the primary targets of our affection. Our desire for the perfect house, attractive clothes, that antique for our collection, or the latest technological gadget can become so important to us that our focus is turned away from Christ. Our love for things and the thrill of a bargain can become a driving force in our lives. After all the gathering of material things is over and after the temporary satisfaction is gone, we find ourselves lost, distracted, and purposeless. Our mass consumption has moved us away from the One who knows us best and loves us most. Jesus understood this pitfall and clearly said, "Do not store up for yourselves treasures on earth, where moth and rust destroy, and where thieves break in and steal. But store up for yourselves treasures in heaven, where moth and rust do not break in and steal. For where your treasure is, there your heart will be also" (Matt. 6:19–21).

When Jesus is Lord of our lives, He becomes the primary target of our affection. When Jesus is Lord of our lives, He is our master, boss, and leader. His purpose is far-reaching, because as we love Him first and give Him first place in our lives, we are better worshipers, wives, mothers, servants, and people. Our lives bring glory and honor to Him.

We live in a world of mass-marketing, advertising, and materialism. Marketers and advertisers of every company from Maybelline to Toyota to Burger King are experts at getting our attention. They compete for our interest—even our affection—for their products. You and I are in danger of allowing the culture we live in to influence us to the point where we become numb to the fact that many bad and good things can divert our relationship with God and our worship of Him. These influences compete for our focus. Worship will not happen unless we intentionally set our mind's attention and heart's affection on God.

Spiritual Transformation

Worship is a response to God. So how do we respond to God in worship? By setting the whole pursuit of our life on God. Romans 12:1–2 says not to conform to the world, but to be transformed by the renewing of our minds. As we intentionally set our focus completely on God, we will be changed—transformed—and we will know God's will, that which is good, pleasing, and perfect.

The Message paraphrase of Romans 12:1–2 says, "So here's what I want you to do, God helping you: Take your everyday, ordinary life—your sleeping, eating, going-to-work, and walking-around life—and place it before God as an offering. Embracing what God does for you is the best thing you can do for him. Don't become so well-adjusted to your culture that you fit into it without even thinking. Instead, fix your attention on God. You'll be changed from the inside out. Readily recognize what He wants from you and quickly respond to it. Unlike the culture around always dragging you down to its level of immaturity, God brings the best our of you, develops well-formed maturity in you."

That passage describes what it means to live a lifestyle of worship. What is it that hinders you in your worship? What do you bring to the worship table that you think is not good enough to offer God? Romans 12:1–2 reminds us to place our lives before God as an offering. As we do this, transformation takes place and we are able to understand His will. We experience an inner, spiritual change in our lives that only God can make possible. Many people don't understand this truth. Sometimes it is even the church-going people of our day that fail to allow God to open their eyes to the truth of who He is and His concern for all of our hearts.

Jesus consistently dealt with and confronted the religious people of His day. The Pharisees and Sadducees were church-going people who were concerned with doing what was right. However, they were much more concerned with "the letter of the law" than with the reality that God is much more concerned with our hearts, our motives, and our sincerity. The Pharisees and Sadducees that Jesus dealt with were also interested in power and control. Their trust was in people and in the law, rather than God. As you and I look around us and even in our churches, we see a lot of folks who are the Pharisees and Sadducees of our day. Perhaps we are they!

I sometimes see church-going Christian women who are missing true worship for the same reason that the Pharisees and Sadducees did. They are "set in their ways" and tradition or routine has become more dominant in their lives than a fresh and growing relationship with God. I know women who have sat under the teaching of some of the finest Bible teachers for many years. They have a good sound knowledge of God's word. But for some reason, their knowledge fails to connect with their heart. The full extent of their relationship with God is simply going to church and praying before meals…and if there is a crisis in their lives, they will pray to God.

Now those things are good, but it appears to me that they haven't been willing to embrace the truth and allow God to change them from the inside out. This is the transformation described in Romans 12:1–2. These women are more concerned with themselves than with God on a daily basis. Perhaps God really wants to do some incredible things in their lives, but they will never see or understand this because they are stuck in traditions that are comfortable to them. For whatever reason, they may not want to see, hear, or understand what God really wants to do with them and what it really means to follow Him.

Living a life without passion or love for God makes our lives, as Paul says, a noisy gong or a clanging cymbal. When we are so consumed with ourselves and unable to put our mind's attention and heart's affection on God, our attempts at worship are just a bunch of noise. We miss what Jesus really wants for us—to know Him, to love Him, to trust Him, to worship Him.

Some years ago, a friend gave me a small book called *The Practice of the Presence of God*. It is by Brother Lawrence, a man who led a simple life and continuously fixed his eyes on Jesus. The book reveals that whatever he did, whether washing dishes or cleaning floors, Brother Lawrence was aware of God's presence. All he did was unto the Lord. Near the end of his life, Brother Lawrence was asked how he spent his time. He replied, "Blessing God, praising God, adoring Him, and loving Him with all my heart. That is our whole purpose…to adore God and to love Him, without worrying about the rest."

Is your life given over to God in such a way that everything you do gives Him glory? Are you aware that you can do everything in life in worship of Him? When you do, God will find in you, one whom He seeks, a true worshiper. 🕸

You Are My God

Based on Psalm 139 and
Lamentations 3:22–23

I read in your word that You delight in me,
That you know my thoughts, my hurts and
fears.
You know my days, my life, my years.
I'm amazed to know Creator of the world
would know my heart,
And God of all the universe would give me a
new start.

You are an awesome God, a holy God,
A loving and gracious friend.
You're almighty God, powerful God,
With greater love than we can comprehend.
You are powerful and strong, gentle and kind,
Caring and true, You make each day new
And You never fail to love me.
You are my God.

"You are My God"
(Sarah S. Groves)
From *Certain Call*
© 2000 Woman's Missionary Union
Birmingham, Alabama
Used by permission.

Chapter Four

TEMPTATION
TO TURN

Do you remember the old hymn, "Yield Not to Temptation"? The lyrics go like this:

> *Yield not to temptation*
> *For yielding is sin.*
> *Each victory will help you*
> *Some other to win.*
> *Fight manfully onward*
> *Dark passions subdue.*
> *Look ever to Jesus*
> *He will carry you through.*[1]

What a great hymn! And what great biblical principles that we so desperately need today!

Every proper response we have to God is an act of worship. And yet our worship is so easily destroyed when we fall to the temptation of sin. It may help to be reminded from the very beginning that our Lord Jesus knows and understands our temptation, because He himself suffered temptation while living here on earth. The four Gospels record the temptation of Jesus Christ, and each shows us that Jesus was able to overcome Satan's temptation with a clear knowledge of the word of God. Satan could not and did not influence Jesus' knowledge of and relationship with the word of God. After all Jesus Christ is the word of God made flesh (John 1:14). To deny the word would be to deny Himself. That He will not do (2 Tim. 2:13).

Let's take a look at a few New Testament passages concerning temptation. We learn from the writer of Hebrews that since Jesus Christ was tempted in that which He suffered, He is able to come to the aid of all those who are tempted (Heb. 2:18). Furthermore, Christ is now our High Priest at the very throne of God, sympathizing with our weakness, ever living to make intercession for us. For Jesus is not a High Priest who cannot sympathize with our weaknesses, but one who has been tempted in all things as we are, yet without sin (Heb. 4:15).

Jesus knew that we all would be susceptible to temptation. As He prayed in the garden just before His arrest and crucifixion, He saw His disciples sleeping at a very crucial hour and warned them twice to watch and pray that they would not enter into temptation (Luke 22:40,46). He even taught us to pray that we would not be lead into temptation, but delivered from evil (Matt. 6:13).

And how we must remember 1 Corinthians 10:13: "No temptation has overtaken you but such as is common to man; and God is faithful, who will not allow you to be tempted beyond what you are able, but with the temptation will provide the way of escape also, that you may be able to endure it."

We learn from James that God does not tempt. James explains that temptation comes when we are carried away by our own lust. Then, when lust is conceived, it gives birth to sin. When sin is accomplished, it gives birth to death (James 1:14–15).

When we allow God's Spirit to guide us into these and all truths, we find that our heart's desire is to respond appropriately and to be strengthened in our life of true worship. We want to stand strong in times of temptations so that sin does not defile our relationship to God. Now that we understand that every proper response to God is an act of worship, it is only fitting that we continue by taking a look at the first relationship with and response to God.

In the Beginning

It should be no surprise to you that the first worshipers were the first people, Adam and Eve. People have always worshiped God. People have always responded to God. People have always heard the voice of God and have always had a choice as to what their response to God would be.

You can read in Genesis 1–3 the story of the first family of the Bible and clearly see that they knew the voice of God and experienced unbroken fellowship with Him. Adam and Eve enjoyed a wonderful life of worship…until they chose to respond inappropriately to what God had spoken. I bet they wished that they had known then what we know now. Their decision to eat of the tree of the knowledge of good and evil, after God had instructed them not to, was an improper response to God. This response is what severed complete fellowship with God. Their disobedience created the great divide that exists today between God and humankind (Rom. 5:12). That separation is called sin. Sin is acting independently of God.

This family that had once known perfect fellowship with God and had lived every day in response to their God, now found themselves hiding from and totally ashamed of even coming into the presence of the One they had known and loved so deeply.

Consider man's first relationship with God. In Genesis 2, God spoke to Adam. Keep in mind that God initiates a relationship with us, and it is our choice as to how we will respond. So it was for Adam.

Adam had all he needed for "godly living": God's instruction to him and a daily, personal relationship with God (2 Peter 1:3). Adam spent his days responding to God. This man was living a lifestyle of worship. He did not live to please himself, but he lived to please and maintain a relationship with his Creator. Then God gave him a wife. Yeah! Marriage is God's plan, God's design for man and woman. I believe God gave man a helper to come along beside him, to uphold God's truths, and to walk daily in a covenant relationship with man and with God. Now that's the life.

But what happened? It's obvious that Adam had shared God's instructions with his wife. Eve knew that God had commanded them not to eat of the tree of good and evil. God never intended for us to know evil (Jer. 29:11). Yet when the tempter came, the woman entertained "temptation" with a conversation about the validity of what God had said. She also allowed the tempter to attack the character of God. Thirdly, she allowed him to give her a wrong opinion of herself.

God's Word Stands Alone

One of the first mistakes we make that inhibits our life of worship is our questioning the validity of the word of God. There should be no questioning the truth of Scripture. As we learn *how* to study God's word, understanding it becomes much easier. Too often we run to books about the Bible and not to the Bible itself— the perfect word of God.

Satan, the Tempter, knows that if we do not know the word of God, we have absolutely nothing to stand on. You see he knows the Scriptures as well as and probably better than we do. He knows that he is no match for the Word, because it has always defeated him. He knows that God's word and God's name are synonymous, and at the name of Jesus, who is the word of God made flesh (John 1:14), the devil and all his cohorts tremble.

The question is do we know the word of God well enough to stand firm when it is being attacked in our own lives? As you read in chapter 1, we are commanded to study and to know and to be ever increasing in the knowledge of God. God wants us to be victorious, and He knows that when His word is in us we will be valiant warriors.

So what was Eve's problem? Consider the dialogue from Genesis. God said, "but from the tree of the knowledge of good and evil you shall not eat, for in the day that you eat from it you shall *surely* die" (Gen. 2:17).

The tempter asked, "Indeed, has God said, 'you shall not eat from any tree of the garden'?" (Gen. 3:1). Notice he said nothing about dying or separation from God.

Eve answered, "from the fruit of the trees of the garden we may eat; but from the fruit of the tree which is in the middle of the garden, God has said, 'you shall not eat from it or touch it, *lest* you die'" (Gen. 3:2–3).

God said you shall *surely* die. Eve said, *perhaps* you'll die. She questioned the validity of God's words. Satan knew he had an open door. Eve had a head knowledge of God's word, but not a heart knowledge. That's religion. Christianity is not about religion; it is about a relationship with the Most High God.

Once the tempter was able to cause Eve to question the authenticity of what God had said, his second attack was on God's character. He says in verses 4 and 5, "you surely shall not die!" (Now that's a bold face lie and a direct violation to what God had already spoken.) "For God knows that in the day you eat from it your eyes will be opened, and you will be like God, knowing good and evil."

The serpent is basically saying, "Okay, so you think you know what God has said, but do you really believe that God meant it? You're not going to die, you're only going to be like God, and He knows that. He's holding out on you!"

In chapter 1, I mentioned "observation" as a step in understanding the Bible. Through observation we ask the question, "What does God's word say?" The word of God did not have a "firm root" in Eve's heart. We could pause here and survey the possibilities as to why Eve responded the way she did, but for now, it's enough to know that she was not "handling accurately the word of truth" (2 Tim. 2:15).

Her next step in this downward fall was at the level of "interpretation." Instead of fleeing the devil and running to her Creator for clarity and understanding, Eve allowed the tempter to influence her interpretation of God's word. Horrors! Do you see the danger in allowing outside sources to influence us, before we allow God's word to speak to us first?

As you continue to read this story, you will find that Eve ultimately gave in to the tempter, and did the very thing that God had commanded, not suggested, that they not do.

As New Testament believers, we have the Holy Spirit, the resident teacher, living within us, and we must allow Him to teach us what God's word says, as well as what it means. Then and only then will we know how to apply what it says and what it means to our lives.

We will also be able to stand against the schemes of the devil. Because Eve allowed this misinterpretation of the word of God to influence her, her faith in the word of God and in the heart of God began to waver.

If our head knowledge does not become heart knowledge what we have is religion and no relationship with God. That's the way it was with the Pharisees and Sadducees Sarah wrote about in the previous chapter. If we are going to develop a life of worship, then we must allow the Spirit of God to interpret the word of God to us daily. As this relationship grows and intensifies, we will find ourselves living in response to God's truth, and nothing else. Now that's the life.

A Look at Ourselves

Because the tempter was able to get Eve to doubt the validity of God's word and His heart, he was also able to convince her that God was not fair, and that she deserved more than she was getting. He deceived her into thinking more highly of herself than she should have.

Surely we should have a positive self-esteem, and the Bible offers us volumes of wonderful affirmations we should know and hold onto about ourselves. Nevertheless, we should never think that we are in any way equal to God or that we ever will be. That is the lie of the devil.

In Genesis 3:5, look at how many times the devil gets Eve to look at herself and not at God. "For God knows that when *you* eat of it *your* eyes will be opened, and *you* will be like God."

I have read in several books on letter-writing that you should use the person's name to whom you are writing as often as possible. That will keep their attention, and you will better accomplish your purpose in sending the letter. This idea is not new, but it sure has been marketed as a brilliant new idea. It's as old as the devil, and one of his schemes against us is to get us to start thinking selfishly. This is like poison in our souls, because to think that we deserve more is to think that God is not fair. That is a lie. God is just and right, and our goal is to receive the righteousness of God and daily align ourselves with it.

My sweet husband just reminded me that there are only two ways of thinking, God's way or the wrong way. There is nothing in between. Don't fall for the lie. Eve looked at herself through the eyes of the tempter and got a false impression of who she truly was. We have all done this. We women have fallen for too many lies. We have believed that we need a man in our lives and settled for someone out of God's will. We have sought love and settled for impurity. We have been deceived into thinking that our outward beauty and our material possessions are most important.

First Timothy 1:9 says, "But those who want to get rich fall into temptation and a snare and many foolish and harmful desires which plunge men into ruin and destruction."

My sister, God has a great plan for your life, and He is waiting patiently for you to run to Him. He is more than willing and able to take care of you. God is the all-sufficient God. Do not be deceived by things of this world. God is in control. By acknowledging His lordship in all things, you are indeed living a wonderful life of worship. You are responding to God, and not to the world around you.

We know that Eve gave in to the tempter and ate the forbidden fruit. She also gave it to her husband, and he ate as well. Ladies, we must be extremely careful with every decision we make, because those around us, in one way or another, will be affected by our decisions. Adam and Eve's act of disobedience severed their intimacy with God. Our acts of disobedience separate us from God, as well.

However, God is gracious, and full of mercy. God also knows how to rescue the godly from temptation (2 Peter 2:9). Knowing the sinful state that humankind is now in, God still comes to us. God comes as a wonderful counselor, asking all the right questions, so that we can confess our sin before Him. God offers us the opportunity to declare that He is indeed right, and every other opinion is wrong.

We also see from Genesis that Adam blames God and Eve for his sin, and Eve blames the serpent. Ladies, there comes a time in every life that we must stop blaming others for our own personal sin.

God's Victory

God deals with Adam and Eve later. First, he curses the tempter. Remember that the devil is defeated. He is cursed of God, and yes, he is God's enemy as well as ours.

God's punishment for Adam and Eve was banishment from

their beloved garden and from their communion with God. Devastating. Yet even then God promised us a Deliverer, a Redeemer, a Savior, the Lord Jesus Christ. There was hope for Adam and Eve, and there is hope for us. For God has indeed sent us a deliverer, His Son, the Lamb of God who was slain, providing us access back into the presence of God.

Don't let anything or anyone steal faith in God's truth from your heart. Without it you really have nothing. With it, you have all that you need for a life of worship.

Just as God came to the garden to restore Adam and Eve, He comes to us today to seek and to save that which was lost. He comes to give us life and to destroy the works of the devil (Luke 19:10, John 10:10, 1 John 3:8).

The story of Adam and Eve does not end here. You may be wondering why God banished Adam and Eve from the garden if His plan was to restore their relationship with Him? Great question! I asked it for years, and in my studies I have learned that God's sending them away was an act of mercy and grace. For in the garden there was not only the tree of good and evil, which they had, in disobedience, taken from, but there also was the tree of life.

Now that Adam and Eve were aware of both good and evil, they would have eaten from the tree of life as well. Had God allowed them to do this, they would have to spend eternity outside of the will of God. That's hell—literally! God created hell for the devil and his cohorts, not for mankind (Matt. 25:14). His plan for man-kind is eternal restoration back into His holy presence. God, in His infinite grace, banished Adam and Eve from the garden and stationed the cherubim and the flaming sword that turned every direction to guard the way to the tree of life. The good news is that the day will come when our struggle with good and evil will be done away with. Yes the day will come when we will only know good and the presence of God. Through faith in the Seed, the Lord Jesus Christ, when we pass from this life to eternal life, our struggle with sin will be eternally over, and we will forever live a wonderful lifestyle of worship. Now there's the victory.

Keep Out the Garbage

A story goes that a father would not allow his children to see a particular movie. The kids protested that the movie didn't have *a lot* of foul language, violence, or nudity, and that their father was being too strict. He was uncomfortable with the amount it did have and did not want his children to be affected by it.

The father wanted to show the children that he was not trying to punish them, but to protect them. He called the family together for an evening of fun, and asked the children to help him make brownies. Everyone had fun making brownies. The kids were still pouting that they did not get to see the movie, but this little family time seemed to be working.

That is until the father decided to add a small can of dog food to the brownie batter. The kids were beside themselves. They could not believe that their father would put dog food in their brownies and expect them to eat it. The father explained that he would be very careful to spread it around so that they only got a very small piece of dog food in each brownie. He further explained that there was such a small amount of dog food in the whole pan of brownies, that perhaps their pieces would not have any at all.

The kids were appalled that their father would even suggest that they eat a brownie that might have dog food in it. This discussion went on until the brownies were out of the oven and ready to be eaten. By now the protest was heated, and the kids were vehemently opposed to even touching the brownies.

The father explained that the movie they wanted to see was just like the brownies they refused to even touch. The movie, like the brownies, had just a little "bad stuff" spread throughout. The father explained to his children that he felt the same way about the movie that they felt about the brownies. The small amount of garbage in the movie tainted the whole thing and made it unsuitable for them to watch—just as the brownies were unsuitable to eat.

Friends, this is the approach we must take with any and everything that would come into our lives and violate the holiness of God. Let us reject the "little bit" of dog food that the world and the devil keep handing us. Run to our Savior, so that nothing will impede this wonderful lifestyle of worship.

Some Verses to Think About

Hebrews 11:37–12:2

"They were stoned, they were sawn in two, they were tempted, they were put to death with the sword; they went about in sheepskins, in goatskins, being destitute, afflicted, ill-treated, ([men and women] of whom the world was not worthy), wandering in deserts and mountains and caves and holes in the ground.

"Therefore, since we have so great a cloud of witnesses surrounding us, let us also lay aside every encumbrance, and the sin which so easily entangles us, and let us run with endurance the race that is set before us, fixing our eyes on Jesus, the author and perfecter of faith, who for the joy set before Him endured the cross, despising the shame, and has sat down at the right hand of the throne of God."

Hebrews 4:16

"Let us therefore draw near with confidence to the throne of grace, that we may receive mercy and may find grace to help in time of need."

Ephesians 6:11–13

"Put on the full armor of God, that you may be able to stand firm against the schemes of the devil. For our struggle is not against flesh and blood, but against the rulers, against the powers, against the world forces of this darkness, against the spiritual forces of wickedness in the heavenly places.

Therefore, take up the full armor of God, that you may be able to resist in the evil day, and having done everything, to stand firm."

James 4:7–8

"Submit therefore to God. Resist the devil and he will flee from you. Draw near to God and He will draw near to you."

Colossians 3:16

"Let the word of Christ richly dwell within you, with all wisdom teaching and admonishing one another with psalms and hymns and spiritual songs, singing with thankfulness in your hearts to God."

Yield Not
To Temptation

To Him that o'er cometh

God giveth a crown

Thro' faith we shall conquer

Though often cast down

He who is our Savior

Our strength will renew

Look ever to Jesus

He will carry you through.

Chapter Five

HEART OF THE MATTER

As we discussed in the last chapter, Adam and Eve, the first family of creation, enjoyed a wonderful life of worship, twenty-four hours a day, in the presence of Elohim, their Creator God. That is until they chose to disobey God and partake of the tree of good and evil. Their disobedience is called sin, and it was this act of sin that severed them and the entire human race from the presence of God (Rom. 5:15). God is holy, and in His presence nothing contradicts or violates His holiness.

Adam fully understood that the penalty for his action was death. For God had said that "You must not eat from the tree of the knowledge of good and evil, for when you eat of it you will surely die" (Gen. 2:17). Therefore, when Adam heard the foot-steps of God in the garden, he hid himself from the presence of God, knowing his punishment would be death.

But Adam and Eve did not know the boundless love of God and the amazing grace of God. Though the spiritual decay of humankind began at the moment Adam and Eve disobeyed the word of the Lord, God, in His great mercy, planned to redeem His children. The Lord intended to seek and to save that which was lost and to destroy the works of the devil.

Instead of destroying the lives of Adam and Eve, God took the life of innocent animals, covered Adam and Eve in those skins, and offered them access into His presence again. This sub-stitutionary death ritual became an act of worship for Adam and Eve. They learned from this experience that even though they deserved death and total banishment from the presence of God, God was willing to accept the death of another in their place. They also knew that they were to offer that life with the clear understanding that the wrath of God had been poured out on the life of another, as payment for the sin they had committed. They now knew that they were to come clean before the Lord, not blaming each other or the devil for their sin, but with a broken and repentant heart. Then they would receive God's forgiveness and fellowship with Him again.

Adam and Eve also believed in the promised "seed" (Gen. 3:15) who would come and deliver them, not only from the penalty and power of sin, but ultimately from the presence of sin, back into a perfect relationship with God their Creator.

Worship vs. Workship

In Genesis 4, it is recorded that Adam and Eve had two sons, Cain, the older, and Abel, the younger. Adam and Eve probably believed that Cain was the promised "seed" that would atone for their sin and bring them back into the relationship they had known with God in the garden. At the birth of Cain, Eve exclaimed, "With the help of the Lord I have brought forth a man." Theologians agree that an alternate translation of this is "With the help of the Lord I have brought forth a God-man." The name *Cain* indicates possession. Adam and Eve believed their son to be a cherished child, for he was indeed the fulfillment of the promise of God. They were sadly mistaken!

They held on so tightly to their belief that Cain was the redeemer, that when they gave birth to their second son, Abel, his life to them was insignificant. This is reflected in his name, for the name *Abel* means vanity or emptiness. The name *Abel* signifies no expectation or brevity. From this we assume that Adam and Eve had no expectations for Abel, and that because he was insignificant in their eyes, his life would even be shortened. Nevertheless, Adam and Eve taught both their boys about the fall, and what it would take for them to regain access into the presence of God.

Go with me a moment to a "what if." What if Adam and Eve told Cain that he was the God-man and that he would save them all from the terrible state that they were in? What if Cain had been made to think that he was the "one" who would indeed bruise the serpent's head and bring restoration to his family and to all mankind? How do you think this information could have affected Cain's heart toward God or toward his brother?

What if they had told Abel that he was a wretched sinner and that he needed the mercy of God to save him, and his sacrifice to God had better be offered with the right heart? How do you think this would have affected Abel's heart toward God?

If this were the case, and it's not an unlikely scenario, then what an awkward position for parents to put their children in. No one child is more significant than any other child. We are all fearfully and wonderfully made by God, and children are a gift of the Lord (Psalm127:3–5).

Though this family had its areas of being dysfunctional, they still were a family that worshiped God. They had organized times of worship, for Scripture says in Genesis 4:3, "So it came about in the course of time." This indicates that this time was marked out for a special season of worship. This is the first mention of organized corporate worship in the word of God. Take special note that Adam and Eve most likely taught their sons that worship indeed involved a sacrifice, a life or that which sustains life.

In Genesis 4 we see both sons bringing an offering to the Lord, but the Lord had regard for one and not for the other.

Genesis 4:3–5 says, "So it came about in the course of time that Cain brought an offering to the LORD of the fruit of the ground. And Abel, on his part also brought of the firstlings of his flock and of their fat portions. And the LORD had regard for Abel and for his offering; but for Cain and for his offering He had no regard. So Cain became very angry and his countenance fell."

God had regard for Abel and for His offering, but for Cain and his offering, the Lord had no regard. The question is why? Why would God regard one offering and not another? I mean, they both showed up for church and gave to the offering. That is a big deal for many people. As long as they do their duty they think they are living a life of worship. This is the sad mistake of Cain and far too many Christians.

Oh my friend, if we think that God is only looking at what we give or what our outward actions are in response to Him, we are deceiving ourselves. God not only sees our gifts and our service, but He also sees our hearts. With God, the heart of the matter is the matter of the heart (1 Sam. 16:7).

Worship involves gaining a correct estimation of the worthiness of something or someone and then giving proper honor, praise, and respect in response. The worship of God involves the heart of a person in pursuit of the worthiness of God, followed by acts of love and obedience.

Cain's heart was not in pursuit of the worthiness of God. He had a self-righteous heart that would not allow him to have a correct estimate of who God was. Therefore His sacrifice was with regard to himself and not to God.

A correct knowledge of the worthiness of God will cause us to have the highest esteem for God. Then we are less likely to allow what I call the "dailyness" of life to thwart our life of worshiping God. I have seen in my own life that the more I know God through His word, the deeper our relationship, the better my response. I guess there is no getting around it. If God is to have regard for our worship, then our worship must have regard for God.

One of the greatest questions my husband and I are learning to ask each other is the same question I am learning to ask God: "How can I serve you?" This is the heart God is looking for— one that reverently comes before Him in pursuit of what brings pleasure to His holy heart.

What a way to start the day, by simply going to God and asking, "How can I serve you?" My favorite way to start the day is by simply going to God with an empty page and allowing Him to write on it what He would have me to do. God is not Santa Claus, nor is He some stock boy in a warehouse waiting to fill our order. Yes, He cares about our needs and wants us to cast all our cares on Him. However, the proper way to approach Him is by seeking His *face*, not His *hand* (2 Chron. 7:14).

In every sacrifice—that is, in all of our worship—God's desire is for a heart that is ready and willing to please Him fore-most. He is looking for hearts that long for Him. When the heart of the sacrifice is pure, then God receives the sacrifice. I hope the picture is getting clearer. What we do and what we give matters only when that service comes from a "willing to please" heart.

The first Christmas we were married, I got my husband everything I wanted him to have and a few things he wanted. He was very gracious, but I could tell by the expression on his face that he was much more pleased with the gifts that he had asked for. The other gifts really were for me. They were nice clothes and "stuff" that would make him look good, but really, they were to make me look good.

Many times, this is how we give to God. We bring Him what we want Him to have, in order that we look good. We would bring so much more pleasure to His heart if we would bring to Him what He has asked of us. God does not want or need our stuff. His desire is to have a relationship with us. His desire is to place His Holy Spirit within us that He might be our God and that we might indeed be His holy people. Once we align ourselves with God—that is once we give Him first place in our hearts as Master—then and only then will we bring to Him the gift that He truly desires from us, a faithful heart.

The problem with Cain's sacrifice was his heart. His offering, his sacrifice was without regard to the holiness and faithfulness of God. In verse 4 we see that Cain's brother Abel brought an offering of the firstlings, indicating the best, of his flock and of their fat portions. By bringing God his best (and God took time to make special note of this in His word), Abel showed forth his faithful heart toward God. He considered God worthy of his best and foremost. Abel was aligned with God. He saw God as Master and himself as servant. He sought to please God. His heart, in pursuit of the worthiness of God, led him to bring the best he had to God. God then received him as well as his sacrifice.

I cannot help but think that if someone worships God like this, she must live like this. True worship is never scripted. It is always from the heart, led by the Spirit of God. The heart of the matter is indeed the matter of the heart.

Repentant Heart

Know that God did not leave Cain in a state of rejection. God offered him the opportunity to be restored, but Cain's prideful and arrogant heart rejected the love of God. Let's finish the story.

Genesis 4:5 states, "But for Cain and for his offering He had no regard. So Cain became very angry and his countenance fell." Cain became bowed, defensive with God. Still God offered him the opportunity to repent and come clean before Him.

"Then the LORD said to Cain, 'Why are you angry? And why has your countenance fallen? If you do well, will not *your countenance* be lifted up? And if you do not do well, sin is crouching at the door; and its desire is for you, but you must master it.'" (Gen. 4:6–7).

Oh my friend, listen carefully to the word of the Lord. His word stands today just as it did in the days of Cain. If our countenance has fallen because of sin, God offers a solution. "Do well!" He is not asking us to perform, but He is asking us to allow His word, by the power of His Spirit in us, to change the wrong that He reveals; then our lives and service will be pleasing to Him. Only after we have seen the error of our ways will we begin to seek truth and allow it to change our hearts. The sum of God's word is truth (Psalm 119:160). If a hard heart persists, sin is crouching at the door, and its desire is for you. Sin desires to destroy your life and relationship with the Almighty. Give no place to it—repent. Run in the opposite direction of sin, and God will save you from the coming judgement. You must master sin. If not, sin will master you (Rom. 6:16).

Look at Genesis 4:8: "And Cain told Abel his brother. And it came about when they were in the field, that Cain rose up against Abel his brother and killed him."

Sin had mastered Cain for he rose up against a righteous man (Matt. 23:35) and killed him. It has been said and it is so true, that sin will take you farther than you ever wanted to go. It will cost you more than you ever wanted to pay, and will keep you longer than you ever wanted to stay. Repent. Change your mind. Go the other way in your heart, in your mind, and in your actions.

The Lord comes again and offers Cain the opportunity to repent, but once again Cain is arrogant and prideful (Gen. 4:9–16). Judgement falls on Cain. Cain is cast out of the presence of the Lord. Eternal separation from God is called death. Cain was dead even though he was still alive. He was indeed a dead man walking. How horrible! Sin took him farther than this son of Adam probably ever thought he would go. It cost him much more than he wanted to pay. It cost him his family, his relationship with God, and ultimately his life. Are you in bondage to sin? Call on the name of the Lord. Let Him forgive you, heal you, and restore you unto Himself again. There is the heart of the matter. There you will rediscover true worship. ✵

I Give You My Heart

This is my desire
To honor You
Lord with all my heart
I worship You.

All I have within me
I give You praise
All that I adore
Is in You.

Lord I give You my heart
I give You my soul
I live for You alone
Every breath that I take
Every moment I'm awake
Lord have Your way in me.

"I Give You My Life"
(Reuben Morgan)
© 1995 Reuben Morgan/Hill Songs Publishing
(ASCAP). 65 Music Square W., Nashville, TN 37203
/Integrity's Hosanna! Music (ASCAP)
1000 Cody Rd., Mobile, AL 36695
All rights reserved. Made in the USA
Used by permission.

Chapter Six

Right Kind of Heart

Alicia wrote in the last chapter about the "heart of the matter." We know that God is concerned with our inward motives and sincerity, not our outward accomplishments. I have seen examples of pure hearts in people I know. Perhaps you have, too. These are the hearts that lead to true worship.

During college, I was a summer missionary in beautiful Lake Placid, New York. Surrounded by gorgeous mountains and lakes, this former site of the Olympics was full of athletes in training and people enjoying the outdoors. I was part of a ministry team and our main assign-ment was music evangelism. We rehearsed and prepared a music program through which we shared the good news of Jesus Christ. We enjoyed the God-given satisfaction of being united in spirit and one in purpose.

Early in our rehearsing and planning of the music program, we discovered that one of the male summer missionaries was tone deaf. In other words, he had difficulty hearing and singing the tones and pitches of songs. Eddie was aware of this problem and the rest of us were quite aware that he seemed to stick out when we sang.

We determined together that Eddie would do some drama in the music program—something that suited his gifts and abilities well. However, I watched Eddie struggle all summer with questions like, "Why has God led me to this place when I am inadequate for the task? How can God use me since I don't have much to offer Him?"

At the end of the summer, we had a campfire and it was our time of saying good-bye to those on the team. It was a typical campfire experience—roasting marshmallows and singing songs. One person would begin a chorus and the rest would join in. Our hearts were full of joy and fulfillment from a life-changing summer, and we sang to God with passion and sincerity.

As we continued to praise, I heard Eddie's monotone voice bellow out, "I have decided to follow Jesus, no turning back. Though none go with me, I still will follow." The sound of his voice…not so great. His worship of God…beautiful! You see, I knew his heart was committed to the truth that he was singing. Eddie was willing to follow Christ at all cost, even if it meant doing it alone. At that moment, I got a glimpse of what it is like to be fully committed to God and to worship Him with all sincerity and honesty.

I gained an important lesson for life. God is not concerned with how beautiful or pleasing things are on the outside. No matter how lovely the music is to our human ears, God is concerned with the heart of the singer, music-maker, or worshiper. It is not just the external things of our life that bring pleasure or worship to God. He is concerned with what is happening on the inside— the heart, soul, and spirit of the person. God longs for us to worship Him in sincerity and honesty, in spirit and truth. As we approach God in this way, true worship happens.

Eddie showed me the heart of true worship.

A Sincere and Honest Heart

Ask any person the qualities they look for in a friend, and honesty will be one of the first characteristics they mention. We all want friends we can trust, those who will be real. God desires the same of us. God knows us intimately, more completely than any earthly friend we know. He wants us to communicate with Him in honesty.

This involves being honest with ourselves, as well. True worship happens when we are authentic with God.

God is a loving friend who can handle our hardest and most confusing circumstances, our joyous or troublesome emotions, and our difficult and challenging questions. He experienced those emotions, questions, and trying circumstances through His Son Jesus Christ who celebrated and suffered like us during His life on earth. In his book, *Reflections on the Gospel of John*, Leon Morris says, "In our worship, we must always keep in mind the truth that we cannot deceive God. We can deceive our neighbors and we can deceive ourselves. But God always knows whether our worship is 'in spirit and truth' or whether it is a sham." We worship and serve almighty God who sees and understands much more of our lives than we will ever see or understand. He sees the whole of us. God delights in His children as we come to Him in honesty and sincerity.

In Spirit and Truth

One of the most precious teachings from Christ on the matter of worship is found in John 4. Jesus' relationship and conversation with a woman He met at a well was and is significant. His initiation of a relationship and conversation with the woman cut through long-standing traditions, overcame existing prejudices, and gave new life to a woman without purpose.

It was a routine and, perhaps, a daily task for women in those days to go to a well and draw water for their basic needs and the needs of their families. (By the way, can Jesus get your attention in your daily routine tasks? Do you give your daily life and tasks as an expression of worship to Him? Are you willing for Him to transform your life just as He did for the woman in this story?) It was at this spot where Jesus initiated a relationship with the woman. Seemingly tired and hot, Jesus began a conversation with a woman who we discover had led a difficult life. We do not know the woman's name, but we do know that she was not respected. During her life she had had five husbands and was currently living with another man. Not the model citizen by any means, this Samaritan woman was stunned to even be asked a question by a Jewish man, much less have a conversation with him. Here again, we see a beautiful picture of God's grace and His unconditional, redeeming, life-changing love.

At the time of this story, Jews and Samaritans were sharply divided over the issue of worship. Jews believed the best place to worship God was at the temple in Jerusalem. Samaritans built their own temple on a mountain and believed that it was the best place to worship.

In the discussion between Jesus and the woman, He clearly knows everything about her, including her past and present sinful ways. Yet Jesus continues to pursue her with the love of God. He does not condemn her, but reveals more of who He is with each piece of the conversation. The woman recognizes Jesus as a prophet so she probes for His opinions on the topic of worship. She claims that "her people" worship on the mountain, but "his people" say they must worship at another place. There were obvious barriers and prejudices between "her people" and "his people."

Jesus said something so important for us to understand. "A time is coming and has now come when the true worshipers will worship the Father in spirit and truth, for they are the kind of worshipers the Father seeks. God is spirit, and His worshipers must worship in spirit and in truth" (John 4:23–24). Jesus helped the woman see that the time to worship is now. To paraphrase, He was saying, "God is here and I am He! The Messiah stands before you and true worship is not dependent on a place, but on knowing Me and understanding you can worship Me anywhere, anytime."

I grew up in the church. I can't remember a time when

church was not a big part of my life. My parents are ministers, and my husband is a minister. I am a seminary graduate, involved in ministry, and often a worship leader on various occasions. I have heard people talk and pray about the importance of worshiping in spirit and truth. Yet I struggle to understand what Jesus really meant when He said these important words.

In my quest to understand what it means to worship in spirit and truth, here is some of what I have discovered. "In spirit" means that God is not confined to material ways, things, or places. Yieldedness to the Holy Spirit, acknowledging the Holy Spirit's presence, allowing the Holy Spirit to speak to us and guide us in worship must be a priority if true worship is to occur. The Samaritan woman thought the issue of worship had to do with the place where you worship. Jesus pierced through that opinion to help us see that worship is not dependent on a place or other material things. We can worship God anywhere, anytime. God is Spirit and we are to worship Him in spirit. I have heard it said that a person's spirit is the "highest part of us." It is the place where our highest dreams, thoughts, ideals, and desires reside. When we worship in spirit, this "highest part of us" meets with the Spirit of God. Worship is a spiritual experience.

In her book *Enter His Gates,* Eleanor Kreider says "The presence of the Holy Spirit makes all the difference in our worship. The Holy Spirit allows Jesus' words to come alive. The Spirit changes our hearts and energizes our wills. The Spirit can enliven our forms of worship to enable joy and spontaneity. The Spirit breaks through human limitations, and links us with God."

To worship "in truth" means to be sincere and honest, as well as with an understanding of what the truth is. When we worship in truth, we are worshiping with complete authenticity. We also worship with an understanding (spiritual, intellectual, and emotional) of the truth of who God is. So when we worship, we sincerely approach God—who is, who was, and who will forever be. We recognize and understand God is worthy of worship, and we are able to respond to the truth of who God is.

Jesus shows us in His conversation with the Samaritan woman that God knows us intimately. While the world focuses on the externals of life, God is concerned with the inside, the heart and core of who we are. He knows our motives, our life circumstances, and personal issues that we bring with us as we worship Him. He is pleased, honored, and glorified when we come to Him in honesty and truth.

For a true worship experience, Jesus says we must worship in spirit and in truth. We cannot have one without the other if true worship is to happen.

A Loving and Adoring Heart

Developing a relationship with God is like falling in love with your sweetheart. I was first interested in my husband, Mark, for several reasons and I wanted to get to know him better. As our relationship developed, we learned to share and open our lives to each other. Our love grew and we were more comfortable being open and honest. We made spending time together a priority. Mark became a strong focus in my life. I made decisions based on my relationship with him.

God wants us to love Him like I have just described. As we grow in our love for God, we learn to share our life with Him and we learn more about who He is. Spending time with Him becomes a priority. All decisions we make are based on our relationship with Him.

When religious scholars asked Jesus what commandment was most important, He declared "Love the Lord God with all your heart and with all your soul and with all your strength and with all your mind" (Matt 22:38). *The Message* paraphrases this

Scripture to help us understand that God wants us to love Him with all we are and have: "Love the Lord God with all your passion and prayer and intelligence."

Worshiping God involves having a loving and adoring heart. The heart is intentionally resolved upon knowing and loving God. Because of a loving and adoring heart for God, a person is able to discern when God is at work and that He desires our full attention. A loving and adoring heart is focused on God, despite distractions, and worships God by expressing that love and adoration.

Mary—Offering Her Best

It was an awkward, unexplainable moment. While attending the party of a respected citizen, Jesus was sharing in the lives of those present. Suddenly a disrespected woman appeared, walked toward Jesus, bowed down before Him, and began to worship. The woman, known as Mary, broke a flask of expensive perfume or oil and anointed the feet of Jesus. Wiping His feet with her hair and her tears, she worshiped Christ with love and adoration.

Uncomfortable to say the least, the party participants questioned the woman's presence and, most likely, were even embarrassed by her actions. But Jesus, with full understanding and deep love for all present, responded in grace. In this moment, He taught those who would listen another truth about worship. He affirmed the woman and her act of worship. He taught the others that her worship was good. She was able to express her love and adoration and was not concerned with what others thought. Jesus declared that she would be forever remembered for what she had done (Mark 14:1–9).

Busy Martha, Wise Mary

Mary and Martha, famous sisters of the Bible, show us great truths about worship and the significance of a loving and adoring heart. If you are even partially acquainted with the brief story in Luke 10:38–42, you are aware that Martha was definitely a busy person. She wanted the house clean, the food just right, and all details taken care of to make her guests feel comfortable. You could say that Martha was much like many of us, she wanted to take care of everybody. She really wanted to do things well and liked it when people noticed that she did. There are thousands of women like her. Good women devoted to working hard to make things just right for their family, friends, and themselves.

In this passage, we see that Martha's sister Mary was unconcerned with all that had to be done. I am sure she completely frustrated her sister. After all, isn't it the polite thing to do to help with the most pressing task? There is a vital truth at work here. Mary was able to distinguish *the important from the urgent*. (Do you give in to the urgent before considering what is most important?) Mary was aware that the moment with Jesus was precious. She was in tune with the fact that God was present. Jesus, the Messiah, in her home, and she wanted to give her undivided and focused attention to the Lord.

Martha couldn't stand it any longer! She exclaimed, "'Lord, do You not care that my sister has left me to do all the serving alone? Then tell her to help me' But the Lord answered and said to her, 'Martha, Martha, you are worried and bothered about so many things; but only one thing is necessary, for Mary has chosen the good part, which shall not be taken away from her'" (Luke 10:40–42).

True, we all have special gifts and abilities that God uses for His glory. Martha could have had the gift of hospitality, while Mary had another. What concerns me when I consider this Scripture is that I know a lot of Marthas and very few Marys. Very few women will let pressing or urgent details be set aside momentarily to focus on the most important concern—to love and worship God, to sit at His feet, to be in His presence, to spend time with Him, and to know Christ more intimately. Very few have nurtured their relationship with God to have such discernment.

God desires our love and worship. When our lives are full of busyness, worry, or responsibility, it hinders us and we are guilty of not choosing what is best, what God wants for us. Jesus said, "'Martha, Martha, you are worried and upset about many things, but only one thing is needed. Mary has chosen what is better, and it will not be taken away from her.'" Mary chose what was best. She chose to set her gaze on God; she had a loving and adoring heart.

Choose to make the important, rather than the urgent, a priority. Set your gaze upon God. Look into His eyes. Feel His presence. Know His love for you. Worship Him.

A Willing and Open Heart

For centuries, God has used ordinary people for extraordinary purposes. Scripture reminds us that God uses what is foolish in the world's view to shame those the world considers wise. Often, God uses people who are deemed unattractive or lacking in talent and skill to bring great glory to Himself. Scripture shows us that God's power is great in our weakness.

God never asks for perfection, financial success, or earthly awards and achievement. God desires to use people who have a willingness and an openness to what He is doing and wants to do. These are the people through which His great purposes are accomplished.

Being responsive and open to God involves a commitment to His lordship in our lives. It includes a determination to respond to God's Spirit at work in our lives and those around us.

God revealed Himself to the prophet Isaiah in a specific way, and we learn about this in Isaiah 6:1–8.

This vision gives us a glorious picture of what happens when we
worship God:

> In the year of King Uzziah's death I saw the Lord
> sitting on a throne, lofty and exalted, with the train of His
> robe filling the temple. Seraphim stood above Him, each
> having six wings: with two he covered his face, and with
> two he covered his feet, and with two he flew. And one
> called out to an other and said, "Holy, Holy, Holy, is the
> Lord of hosts, The whole earth is full of His glory." And
> the foundations of the thresholds trembled at the voice of
> him who called out, while the temple was filling with smoke.
> Then I said, "Woe is me, for I am ruined! Because I am a
> man of unclean lips, And I live among a people of unclean
> lips; For my eyes have seen the King, the Lord of hosts."
> Then one of the seraphim flew to me with a burning coal
> in his hand, which he had taken from the altar with tongs.
> He touched my mouth with it and said, "Behold, this
> has touched your lips; and your iniquity is taken away
> and your sin is forgiven." Then I heard the voice of the
> Lord, saying "Whom shall I send, and who will go for us?"
> Then I said, "Here am I. Send me!"

Worship involves responding to the truth of who God is. It
involves obedience and a willingness to follow God and surren-
dering to who He is in our lives. The process of worship is
revealed in this passage in Isaiah. It includes the following:

• We become aware of God's holiness and greatness.

> Isaiah saw God sitting on a throne, lofty, exalted.
> The seraphim worshiped Him saying "Holy, Holy,
> Holy, is the Lord of hosts, The whole earth is full of
> His glory." (Isa. 6:1–4)

• We become aware of our sinfulness and our need for forgiveness.

> *After he saw the Lord, Isaiah recognized he was unclean and in need of forgiveness.*
>
> (Isa. 6:5)

• We repent and receive God's forgiveness.

> *God granted forgiveness and renewed Isaiah.*
>
> (Isa. 6:6–7)

• We hear and understand God's call.

> *Isaiah heard God's call and understood his need to share God's message with others.*
>
> (Isa. 6:8)

• We respond to God with obedience.

> *Isaiah willingly responded to God's call.*
>
> (Isa. 6:8)

• God gives guidance as we follow Him in obedience.

> *God responded to Isaiah with specific directions for the task..*
>
> (Isa. 6:9–13)

Note that Isaiah responded with an open and willing heart *before* He knew what task God was calling him to. Isaiah was obedient to God's call, and this was a worshipful and obedient response to a holy, almighty, loving, forgiving God. It is also important to see that when God calls us, He does not leave us alone to figure things out. God provides His guidance. As we trust Him, He shows us the things we need to know and when we need to know them.

You may be able to recall a time when God called you or spoke to you specifically in a worship experience. Those moments are points or markers in your life that help to solidify your faith. As we reflect on those experiences, we become more convinced of God's living presence and power in our lives.

I became a Christian during a worship service at a youth camp. I had not listened to a word the preacher had said, but during the invitation time, the Holy Spirit began to speak to me, and I became powerfully aware of who God is, who I am, and that I had a need for God in my life. All I knew was that I needed to respond to Him and give my life to Him. I wanted Him in my life as Lord and Savior, and during that worship experience, I responded with an open and willing heart.

It was in another worship experience where I heard and understood God's call to ministry. As a fifteen-year-old in another youth camp experience, I made a commitment to God to be available to Him for whatever He had planned for my life. As far as I could see at that moment, I believed God was calling me to ministry. I did not know what kind of ministry or how or where or with whom it would happen. But I responded in obedience to who God was and to what He was doing. I trusted fully in His faithfulness to show me His plans for my life.

God has been faithful to that sincere commitment of a young fifteen-year-old. He has opened more doors and opportunities for ministry than I could have ever dreamed. I have experienced disappointment and discouragement, but God has been unwavering in His grace, goodness, and provision of guidance as I have sought to give my life daily to Him. Ephesians 3:20–21 is a favorite passage of mine, for when we respond to God with willing and open hearts and minds, our infinite and eternal God truly does the amazing. "Now to Him who is able to do immeasurably more than all we ask or imagine, according to his power that is at work within us, to him be glory in the church and in Christ Jesus throughout all generations, for ever and ever! Amen."

Lydia—Business Woman with a Willing and Open Heart

Lydia was among the women who gathered by the river. Paul and others who were serving the Lord began speaking with the women. Described in Scripture as a worshiper of God, Lydia was not aware, at this time, of the truth of Jesus Christ. As Paul shared God's truth with the women, Lydia responded with an open heart and immediately began serving the Lord. She was a working woman, a dealer of purple cloth, as Scripture states. As soon as she became a believer in the Lord, she offered her home to Paul and the others serving with him. Lydia was instrumental in seeing that the ministry of these early Christians was accomplished, and she helped to make it happen because of her willing and open heart.

Mary, Mother of Jesus—A True Worshiper

A young woman, really a teenage girl, is perhaps one of the best examples in Scripture for how we are to approach God in worship. Mary learned that God had chosen her to be the mother of Jesus. In response to this news, Mary exclaimed one of the most beautiful prayers of praise and adoration in Scripture. Luke 1:47–55 is known as the *Magnificat*. Her response to God's movement in her life was not one of unwillingness or giving of excuses.

While she probably had fears and concerns, she focused upon the truth that God called her and that He was in control. Her response was true worship of God with an open and adoring heart.

Mary's song reveals to us a picture of a worshiping heart. She declared her worship of God as she glorified the Lord, rejoiced in God, exclaimed who God was, and declared the wonderful works that God had done and continued to do. Look at the declarations she made about God.

God is her Savior (v. 47).

God has regard for her (v. 48).

God is mighty (v. 49).

God has done great things for her (v. 49).

God's name is holy (v. 49).

God has mercy on those who fear Him (v. 50).

God demonstrates His strength (v. 51).

God scatters the proud (v. 51).

God dethrones the mighty (v. 52).

God exalts the humble (v. 52).

God satisfies the hungry (v. 53).

God sends the rich away empty (v. 53).

God helps His servant (v. 54).

God remembers to be merciful (v. 54).[1]

Mary's heart was open to God, loving towards God, committed to serving Him, worshiping Him, and obediently following Him.

Take some time to express your worship to God. Examine your heart. Are you sincere and honest with God? Do you love and adore Him? Are you open to Him and to how He wants to use your life, your unique personality and gifts? Is obedience to God's work in your life difficult? Are you willing to follow Him even if none go with you?

¹ Hunt, T.W., Walker, Catherine, *Disciple's Prayer Life* (Nashville: LifeWay Press, 1997), 207.

The Samaritan Woman
Sarah S. Groves

A lonely soul, rejected, and hurt,
Full of questions, referred to as "dirt"
She didn't know where her life would go
But there was much more she was about to know.

Going to the well, her mundane task,
A Jewish man saw her and began to ask
"May I have a drink? I'm thirsty and hot.
I don't care that you're from Samaria and I'm not.

If you knew Me, you would know, I offer you a gift.
It's Living Water. It quenches thirst, your burdens
it will lift.
I know your life, joys and pains, your past and
present ways
Today I offer you God's great love. I offer you His grace.

Your people worship on the mountain and mine
another place,
But I have come to share with you good news,
face to face.
God can be found, regardless of location,
He'll give you hope, His peace, and salvation.

God seeks to find true worshipers, who give
Him all their life.
Those who worship in spirit and truth, who lay down
their pride,
In humility, honesty, sincerity, and love,
True worshipers glorify God.
Their lives transformed, they change the world,
For their heart beats with God's.

Chapter Seven

Two Altars of Worship

The day I had no words of worship for God was the same day God required of me my "Isaac." It was the day my doctor told me that I had cancer—the same day, as I mentioned before, when I felt like I was hearing the doctor say, "Alicia, you are going to die, soon." I knew that God was asking me to give Him absolutely everything. Cancer would require of me my health, my husband, my happiness, and my home.

Like God calling Abraham to offer his son Isaac, God asked me to give up what was most precious to me. Unlike Abraham, I was not able to say yes to God. I did not want to let go of anything. All of these things were very important to me and I did not want to give them up to anyone, ever!

For days, I struggled alone with this issue. I was crushed, totally depressed, and my world had come to a screeching halt. I apologize that this is no outstanding testimony, but it is the simple truth. I did not do well at all when my "Isaac" was threatened.

Days passed, and I did not get any better. I had not slept through the night in over a week! I felt awful, and I looked even worse. Very early one morning, spiritually and physically exhausted, I needed so desperately for God to help me, that I dragged myself out of bed and into the living room. There, in total depravity, I fell on my face and released to God my Isaac!

That day, in my heart, I died. I knew that my life was out of my control and was really not my own. I had no choice now but to trust God. I began to say to myself all the things that God had given me to share in concert. The word of God came to me.

"'For I know the plans that I have for you,' declares the Lord, 'plans for welfare and not for calamity to give you a future and a hope. Then you will call upon me and come and pray to me, and I will listen to you. And you will seek me and find me, when you search for me with all your heart. And I will be found by you,' declares the Lord, 'and I will restore your fortunes and will gather your fortunes and will gather you from all the nations and from all the places where I have driven you,' declares the Lord, 'and I will bring you back to the place from where I sent you into exile'" (Jer. 29:11–14).

"For I am confident of this very thing, that he who began a good work in you will perfect it until the day of Christ Jesus" (Phil. 1:6).

"For I know whom I have believed and I am convinced that he is able to guard what I have entrusted to Him until that day" (2 Tim. 1:12).

"Trust in the Lord with all your heart, and do not lean on your own understanding. In all your ways acknowledge him, and he will make your paths straight" (Prov. 3:5–6).

"Therefore we do not lose heart, but though our outer man is decaying, yet our inner man is being renewed day by day. For momentary, light affliction is producing for us an eternal weight of glory far beyond all comparison, while we look not at the things which are seen, but at the things which are not seen; for the things which are seen are temporal, but the things which are not seen are eternal" (2 Cor. 4:16–18).

I also remember some kind words spoken to me during a concert tour in Manila, Philippines. "Out of the seed of sacrifice comes greatness." Once I allowed the word of God to strengthen my heart, then and only then was I able to trust God with my Isaac. The moment I raised the knife, God spoke again.

"Healing comes from knowing who I am." That day, the

Lord Jesus visited with me in a most awesome way, for about four hours. I sat on my couch, which became the lap of God, and allowed the presence of Jesus to heal my soul! That day, His word and His presence brought healing to my emotions. I received the peace of God and was able to bow my knee to His lordship in my life.

Today, I can joyfully say that not only did God heal my soul, He sovereignly healed my body as well. Thank you Father! Right now, at the penning of this chapter, my husband and I are awaiting the arrival of our first baby, a boy, Michael Chandler Garcia! God is so good! The reward is far greater than the sacrifice, my friends.

God gave Richard and me faith when He gave us His word. He gave us faith to let go of the temporal that we might hold on to the eternal. Biblical belief always demands a response. The proper response is always obedience to the faith, obedience to the word.

This is the sacrifice of worship! It is relinquishing what we have in our hands and our hearts, in order that we might hold more firmly to the Giver of every good and perfect gift, God Himself. Nothing and no one in the life of the worshiper can supercede the place of God.

The Altar of Sacrifice

Father Abraham was indeed a great worshiper. He was also known as a man with tremendous faith. Genesis 22 tells the story of God testing Abraham's faith as a true worshiper when He asked him to sacrifice Isaac as a burnt offering.

A burnt offering was a love offering—a voluntary offering. The offering was to be secured upon an altar that was strong and steady for the purpose of total consumption. God asked Abraham to make this kind of offering of his son, his only son whom he loved. This was the son that God had brought into Abraham's life some twenty-five years after the promise. Abraham understood that Isaac carried the seed from which the Messiah would come.

This was the child conceived by the will of God and not by the will of man. Abraham was too old to father a child, but God enabled him and his wife Sarah to have Isaac in their old age. Sarah was ninety and Abraham was one hundred years old when Isaac was born. (I'll bet they were cute at the PTA meetings. Or maybe they home-schooled.)

Nevertheless, their son was a precious promise fulfilled, and God was now asking Abraham to offer Isaac as a burnt offering. Abraham understood that the burnt offering was an act of worship. This offering was to be a total surrender of the gift so that he might hold firmly to the Giver of the gift. Abraham would worship by offering his son, and Isaac would worship by offering his life, for God had spoken.

It is of great importance that I mention that in Genesis 22, the word *worship* is mentioned for the first time in all of the word of God. There is a Principle of First Mention that states that when a significant word like *worship* is first used in the Bible, the principles established within that context of Scripture are carried throughout Scripture.

The context here clearly shows us that worship involves sacrifice, and a burnt offering indicates complete consumption. Genesis 22:6 says, "And Abraham took the wood of the burnt offering and laid it on Isaac his son, and he took in his hand the fire and the knife."

It was Abraham's sacrifice of worship to secure the altar, then to deliberately bind the sacrifice, his son, to that altar. He was then to take the knife and plunge it into the heart of his son. Not only that, he was then to leave him there, to be totally consumed by the fire.

Take special note that in the context of this Scripture we see worship involving a father offering his son, his only son, whom he loved. The son does not argue with the father, he simply trusts. We must also note that Abraham told his young men that both he and Isaac were going to return. "We will worship and we will return" (Gen. 22:5).

Allowing Scripture to interpret Scripture, we are told in Hebrews 11:19 that Abraham believed that God was able to raise men even from the dead. "Abraham assumed that if Isaac died, God was able to bring him back to life again. And in a sense, Abraham did receive his son back from the dead" (New Living Translation).

Abraham believed in the resurrection, a foreshadowing of the resurrection of Christ. Note also that in Genesis 22:4 it says, "On the third day Abraham raised his eyes and saw the place from a distance." Three days after Abraham left to sacrifice Isaac, God did raise Isaac from the dead in Abraham's heart, by offering a ram as a substitute for Isaac's death. "Then Abraham raised his eyes and looked, and behold, behind him a ram caught in the thicket by his horns; and Abraham went and took the ram, and offered him up for a burnt offering in the place of his son" (Gen. 22:13).

I love this next part. Verse 14 says, "And Abraham called the name of the place The Lord Will Provide, as it is said to this day, 'In the mount of the Lord it will be provided.'" This is where we get the name of God, *Jehovah Jireh*. *Jireh* is actually translated "to see." How do we get "provide" out of that? God sees, therefore He foresees, and therefore He provides. Isn't our God awesome?

One more thing! I want you to see the heart of God in response to Abraham's obedient sacrifice. Genesis 22:10–12 says, "And Abraham stretched out his hand, and took the knife to slay his son. But the angel of the LORD called to him from heaven, and said, 'Abraham, Abraham!' And he said, 'Here I am.' And he said, 'Do not stretch out your hand against the lad, and do nothing to him; for now I know that you fear God, since you have not withheld your son, your only son, from Me.'"

God saw Abraham's faith when he stretched out his hand and took the knife to slay his son. The next word is a small but powerful word. It's the word that shows contrast and changes the direction of the action—*but*. *But* the angel of the Lord stopped the sacrifice, for he knew that Abraham loved God more than he loved the son that God had given him.

Friends, God and God alone holds first place in the heart of every true worshiper. He will test us, not tempt us, to show us whether or not our hearts are truly His. God was not tempting Abraham. Genesis 22 is a test. Verse 1 says, "Now it came about after these things, that God *tested* Abraham."

Perhaps God is testing you. Has He shown you those things in your life that have become a priority over Him? Do you have time for everything except time to know God better through the study of His word? What is your sacrifice of worship? What are you placing on the altar as a burnt offering because your love for God is greater? David said in 2 Samuel 24:24, "I will not offer burnt offerings to the LORD my God which cost me nothing."

An *offering* is a contribution. A *sacrifice* is the offering or contribution of a life. What is it that you are holding onto because you see it as your source of life? Is it a job, a relationship, possessions, traditions, religion? Don't be afraid to let go of these things. Holding on is simply idolatry, and idolatry has no place in the life of a worshiper.

Give them to God. He may give them back to you. If He gives them back, know that the second giving holds far greater value than the first (Heb. 10:9). If He does not give them back, then you will know for sure, and will thank God for showing you that you did not need it at all. The life of a true worshiper is characterized by the laying aside of all things for the sake of following Christ (Luke 9:23). Another thing: Genesis 22 is also the place in God's word where He first uses the words *love* and *obey.* The context here shows us that our sacrifice of worship must come from a heart that loves God above all and is obedient to His perfect will.

The summer before we got married, Richard and I began looking for a house. We had only a few days to find something because Richard had to get back to New York, where he lived at the time. After an exhausting search we finally found just the house we were looking for. Having prayed that God would show us His will for a home, we believed this house to be His provision. We had faith He would provide the resources for it. But as the closing on the house came closer, we still did not have the money we needed.

We did not want this house if it was not God's plan, and we laid our will and our desire at the altar of sacrifice every day. Nevertheless, our hearts were encouraged to keep the faith and not give up. Just because things were not as easy as we would have wanted them to be, it did not mean that God was not in it.

Still, I felt discouraged. One day, I ran into my friend Grace—I call her Mamma. Mamma has been young for a lot longer than I have, and her faith in God towers over most that I know. I told her what Richard and I were going through and she spoke words to me that I will never forget. "Alicia, God didn't say you have to have money, He said you have to have faith." This was one of the greatest truths I had ever heard in all my life.

God did provide for us, and we were able to buy the home we loved. But we were tested until our faith was strengthened, and we were able to place the house on the altar. God rewarded our faith and our willingness to sacrifice our desire for His.

My friends, there is nothing more precious in the heart of a true worshiper than God Himself. He alone holds first place. Everything else is received as gifts from a loving and gracious God who sees; therefore, He provides. A great woman of faith once said that she has learned to hold all things loosely so that

God will not have to pry them out of her hands. God cannot fill hands and hearts that are already full. This is the sacrifice of worship. It is letting go of all of our gifts, in order that we might hold firmly to the Giver of every good and perfect gift. Nothing and no one can supersede God's place in the life of the worshiper.

The words of Beth Moore's poem "Trust Me With Your Isaac" from *Whispers of Hope* describe this sacrifice of worship. She ends the poem with the final stanza: "Pass the test, my faithful one; bow to me as Lord. Trust me with your Isaac. See, I am your great reward."

The Altar of Service

Genesis chapter 22 is filled with wonderful Old Testament truths that lead us to Romans chapter 12, where the New Testament reality is revealed. Romans 12:1–2 is the Grand Pause of the book of Romans and must be the Grand Pause of the worshiping life. From this altar the life of the worshiper is lived out. "I urge you therefore, brethren, by the mercies of God, to present your bodies a living and holy sacrifice, acceptable to God, [which is] your spiritual service of worship" (vs.1).

There it is. Our spiritual "service" of worship! The service of worship has nothing to do with the things we busy ourselves with and call service. The service of worship is that we simply present our bodies.

Paul says "in view of God's mercies." That means in view of all that accompanies our great salvation (ponder that for a moment), our response should be giving ourselves to God. Trust Him not only with your Isaac but also with you. When we present our bodies, we present all of who we are, for all we are is contained within the walls of our flesh. The true worshiper takes pleasure in presenting her life to God daily, for His purposes alone.

In Romans 6:11–23 Paul gives us a more in-depth discussion as to what it means to present our bodies to God.

Take a few minutes and read these powerful verses. Then consider with me the kind of sacrifice God is asking of us at the altar of service.

A Living Sacrifice

In the Old Testament there are basically three types of offerings. The sin offering was for atonement, the burnt offering for consecration, and the peace offering for fellowship. The offering or sacrifice that Paul is speaking of in Romans 12:1 is the burnt offering.

The burnt offering was one that was placed on the altar and completely consumed by fire. Nothing was spared. The smoke of this all-consuming fire ascended to God and became a fragrance that was pleasing to Him. Remember Isaac was presented to God as a burnt offering.

The New Testament burnt offering is one where the sacrificer offers her total self— body, soul, and spirit—on the altar of God's grace, in order that her entire life might be consumed with the fire of God's presence. Nothing is spared. This is what Isaac became after God gave the ram to die in his place.

The true worshiper does not compartmentalize her life. She offers it daily and completely to God alone.

A Holy Sacrifice

The word *holy* means set apart or sanctified for sacred or divine purposes. Every true believer has the Spirit of Christ in her. Romans 8:9 says that if anyone does not have the Spirit of Christ, he does not belong to God. The Holy Spirit in us sets us apart for sacred and divine purposes. He makes us holy. The Spirit of Christ in us gives us the power in our self-will to live what God calls a holy life. Consider these verses:

1 Corinthians 3:16–17: *"Do you not know that you are a temple of God, and that the Spirit of God dwells in you? If any man destroys the temple of God, God will destroy him, for the temple of God is holy, and that is what you are."*

1 Corinthians 6:19–20: *"Or do you not know that your body is a temple of the Holy Spirit who is in you, whom you have from God, and that you are not your own? For you have been bought with a price: therefore glorify God in your body."*

2 Corinthians 6:16–18: *"Or what agreement has the temple of God with idols? For we are the temple of the living God; just as God said, 'I will dwell in them and walk among them; and I will be their God, and they shall be My people. Therefore, come out from their midst and be separate,' says the Lord. 'And do not touch what is unclean; and I will welcome you. And I will be a father to you, and you shall be sons and daughters to me,' says the Lord Almighty."*

God requires that the life we present to Him be a holy life, one that is separated from the sinfulness that is in the world. You may want to take a little time here and think about the things you allow in your life that would not bring pleasure to the heart of God. Repent, let go of any idol that may want to dwell in your temple, and allow God to fill that space with Himself. The life of a true worshiper is one that is clean and repentant before a holy God.

An Acceptable Sacrifice

Acceptable here simply means well-pleasing. In this book, Sarah and I are focusing on worship that is well-pleasing to the Lord. First Samuel 15:22 says, "And Samuel said, 'Has the LORD as much delight in burnt offerings and sacrifices as in obeying the voice of the LORD? Behold, to obey is better than sacrifice, *and* to heed than the fat of rams.'" Obedience is what God is after, a truly faithful heart. This is well-pleasing to Him.

Acceptable sacrifices in the Old Testament required attention to a lot of details. I am so glad that God has set us free from all of that. Today, our concern simply needs to be the lordship of Jesus Christ. When Christ is truly Lord and Master, we will find that diligently studying His word is a pleasure. Sin no longer is our master, and we are empowered to resist its temptation. Our hearts are pure and not filled with pride and arrogance.

When we are totally submitted to the lordship of Christ, we say *yes* to giving Him our all, even our beloved Isaac. To obey God delights our soul. We take pleasure in living as acceptable sacrifices to God. The life of a true worshiper is always acceptable to God.

Christ our Sacrifice

Letting go is never easy. In fact, it is always very difficult. And perhaps the most difficult thing a human can be asked to give is a child.

God is a parent. He is the Father of Jesus Christ. God required of Himself the letting go of His son, His only Son, the one He loved—Jesus Christ. Now watch this.

In Philippians 2:6–10 it says that Jesus Christ, being fully God, let go of His identity as God. This did not change the fact that He was still indeed God. Jesus Christ is the God-man. Jesus did not consider equality with God a thing to be grasped, but He emptied Himself, took the form of a bond-servant, and was made in the likeness of a human. Being found in the form of man, Jesus, God, humbled Himself by becoming obedient to the point of death, even death on a cross. Life as a bond-servant was the altar where Christ worshiped for thirty-three years—the altar of service. His death was at God's altar of sacrifice, Calvary's cruel cross.

Here at the cross, Jesus became God's final sacrifice of the old way of worship, and is the first and only sacrifice for the new way—*grace*! No more bulls, no more goats, no more rams. Only the eternal fragrance of Christ being offered up on our behalf, by which we now please God and know His divine presence.

His death on the cross was not only the raising up of the knife, but the plunging in which cost Christ His life. His life became the offering, the sacrifice of worship for our lives. He loved His father more than He loved His own life. Christ is our sacrifice! Let us bow the knee and worship at the same altar as He—the altar of service.

I beg you sister, because of the love and acceptance we have received from God, don't go on throwing yourself away as the slave to sin which leads only to death. But keep on presenting yourself to God daily, and become a slave to His righteousness, which leads to eternal life. Present yourself as one who is dead to her own self-will and is alive to the will of God. Come to Him daily and give your total self to Him, holding nothing back. Keep yourself cleansed from the sin that is in the world. Purpose to do those things that please God. This is where it all begins. Nothing counts for God until you stop here. This is your spiritual "service of worship."

I Offer My Life

All that I am all that I have
I lay them down before You O Lord
All my regrets all my acclaim
The joy and the pain
I'm making them Yours.

Chorus:
Lord I offer my life to you
Everything I've been through
Use it for Your glory
Lord I offer my days to you
Lifting my praise to you
As a pleasing sacrifice
Lord I offer you my life.

Things in the past
Things yet unseen
Wishes and dreams
That are yet to come true
All of my hopes
All of my plans
My heart and my hands
Are lifted to You.

Bridge:
What can we give
That you have not given
And what do we have
That is not already yours
All we possess
Are these lives we're living
And that's what we give to You Lord.

"I Offer My Life"
(Don Moen/Claire Cloninger)
© 1994 Word Music, Inc. (ASCAP), 65 Music Square W.,
Nashville, TN 37203/Integrity's Hosanna! Music (ASCAP), 1000
Cody Rd., Mobile, AL 36695
All rights reserved. Made in the USA.
International Copyright secured.
Used by permission.

Chapter Eight

RIGHT GOD, WRONG WORSHIP

I remember sitting in the Atlanta airport, waiting for a flight to Indianapolis. I was just finishing a sandwich when a lady who had been on the telephone came toward me and looked at me as if she knew me. She squinted her eyes for better focus, and so did I.

Just as each of us was gaining our focus, we realized that we did know each other. She was actually a very close friend of some of my friends, but we knew each other well enough to sit and talk while we waited for our flight to begin boarding. Her first words to me were, "I thought I saw that 'Light' in you." She went on to explain that she had been around angry, frustrated, hassled people all day, but when she saw me, even before she realized who I was, she said to herself, "Now that lady has got the Light."

I am not sure just what my friend saw, but since then, my prayer has been that God would allow that Light to shine so bright in me that people who really need the Light of Christ will see it and be drawn to it.

This really is the prayer of those involved in my ministry. If we are on the phone taking care of business details, writing letters, or actually on the platform delivering our message, we want the Light to shine. We want our feet shod with the gospel of peace, so that wherever our ministry is presented, the peace of God is there.

We want Christ to shine so that those around us will feel the love of God, acceptance from God, the righteous fire of God, and the hope that we have in God. Once we have left a place, we want them to remember the presence of God more than they remember what was said or sung.

This is also our prayer for the church. We pray that when people gather to worship the Lord that the experience is felt in the heart, that they see the Light, and that their lives are changed because they have been in the presence of the Light—the Lord Jesus Christ.

We travel across this country and around the world, and the saddest thing we see is a congregation of believers who are not moved by the presence of God. I often say to the team, "I felt like I was singing to a picture."

Make Room for the Spirit

It's hard to believe how familiar with God we have become. It seems like we have mastered our programming and our lifestyle of churchgoing, and there really is little if any place for God to be God.

I have been told by people who followed me in a program not to allow the Spirit of God to move because they had a flight to catch and they wanted to make sure they had enough time for their presentation. One person told me very emphatically that if the Spirit started to move that I was to ignore it. We needed to stick to the program. I wanted to lash out and let the people there know how I felt about it, but the Spirit of the Lord would not allow that.

I am so glad that that person was an invited guest like I was, and that I was not under her authority. The leaders at this particular event wanted God to move, they had prayed diligently for God to bless us with His presence, and He did just that. I do not remember the presentation at all, but I do remember the cleansing that came to my soul as the Spirit of the Lord came and visited with us. Blessed be the name of the Lord.

I also remember a service in Brooklyn, New York where a very prominent preacher had been invited to speak. During the praise and worship time the Spirit of the Lord moved so powerfully that the pastor of the church gave an altar call and we just prayed and worshiped God for the entire service. At the end of the service, the pastor apologized to the guest preacher and told him he would invite him back at another time. The guest did not mind at all. He too was blessed by the presence of the Lord.

Some may argue that God cannot move like that unless there's preaching from the Bible. Now, I love the word of God and I am a changed person because of the word of God. Nevertheless, I know, from the word of God, that God can do whatever He wants—whenever He wants. I know that He does not live in the little box that most of us put Him in.

We use statements like this to validate the part of the service that platforms us, but the truth is, God does not need any of us. Yet, it is His good pleasure to use us. Yes, we need to receive an offering or go to Sunday School classes, but when God is moving during a song service, a sermon, or altar call…*let Him move! It's His church!*

God moves in my heart in the middle of the night, and I find myself worshiping Him, praying to Him, or just being still and allowing Him to minister to my soul. He moves in my heart when I am cooking a meal, and I just have to stop for a moment and let God be God. Have you ever been driving along listening to a wonderful song or perhaps you were just praising the Lord for His faithfulness in your life, and the Spirit of God filled your heart so much that you just had to pull over and praise the Lord? It's happened to me many times, and I thank God for them all.

You may or may not believe this next story but it is the truth. I was speaking with a concert sponsor about the event where I would sing and bring the message God had given me. No lie, he said to me, "We have to be out by 7:15. We absolutely cannot go over."

I asked him why. I could not think of anything more pressing on a Sunday night than spending time in God's presence with

His people. His response to my question was, "Because we have a big ice cream social planned at 7:30 P.M."

Dead silence.

I think that after the words came out of his mouth, he was a little embarrassed at what he had just said. I could not respond. I just said fine and that I would see him on Sunday.

An ice cream social! An ice cream social! God help us!

Yet this is what I see too much of. There are more and more programs and less and less God. Now I am a great programmer. I get asked to put together praise and worship for large and small events all of the time. I love PowerPoint in a worship service. I use it often. But if a song comes to my heart that is not on PowerPoint, that does not stop me from singing it. Or if I have ten songs on PowerPoint and God says just sing two, I will sing those two until He says stop. It may be a hymn or a praise song, but if it is a truth that God wants us to respond to, we sing it until the Spirit has moved in whatever way He desires.

I know you want to say "Well that's just emotionalism. You're just working yourself up." Believe me, I know the difference between emotionalism and the Spirit of God. Truth is truth, whether it is spoken or sung. True worship has always been and always will be believers responding appropriately to truth. God's word, sung or spoken, is truth. We have fallen for the lie that tells us that we have to entertain people to get them to come to church. People will come to where God is moving.

Read your Bible. Whether they liked Jesus or not, people were always curious about what He was doing. Many followed out of curiosity and became believers. Others clung to religion and fitted themselves for eternity in hell. When we let God be God, people will come.

Where's the Light?

Worship is not business as usual. It's not "sticking to the program," or "be done by such and such a time." Believe it or not, worship is not singing a song. We may sing and praise God but that does not necessarily mean that we have worshiped Him.

Worship is our hearts crying out to God, "Have Thine own way Lord!" It's the faith of the believer allowing the Spirit of God to totally control her life. We sing it, but I am afraid we don't really mean it.

I heard one of my favorite pastors read from Revelation what it would really mean if we prayed and prayed for God to come in majesty, strength, and power. We see Jesus come in this way to John on the island of Patmos. John fell on his face, like a dead man, at the feet of Jesus. The pastor asked how many in his congregation wanted to get in the isles or at the altar and fall on their faces before the Lord. Nobody moved.

You see, we know how to speak "churchanease," and we have got the ritual of going to church or putting together an event figured out, but we have yet to learn how to worship. Many times what we call the praise and worship part of our service is really a well-produced or orchestrated performance by the choir and orchestra. There is little, if any, time for me in the congregation to sing along and invite God to speak to me during the service. I just get to watch the show. A worship service should allow me ample time to engage my heart in the pursuit of the worthiness of God.

We have scared the Light out of some of our pastors. They are paranoid to continue preaching after 12:00 P.M. because they know that "sister so and so" or "brother so and so" will not give in the offering. What is that? If that's the way we run our churches and our worship events, no wonder the church isn't any stronger than it is. No wonder we have lost our saltiness.

Apathy and apostasy seem to plague many worship services. *Apathy* is a lack of feeling (I know we are afraid of that word) or emotion (we are afraid of that one too). It's also a lack of interest or concern. *Apostasy* is an abandonment of a previous loyalty, or a turning away from.

Let's face it, we have gotten very apathetic toward the word of God, therefore we have gotten apathetic in our worship. Apathy leads to apostasy. We learn this in the book of Judges. When we become apathetic towards the word of God, we apostatize, we turn away from following God. Romans 6:16 tells us that we become a slave to that which we obey.

I have to tell you a funny story that I heard in the great state of Kentucky. I was talking with a young preacher friend who had been called to pastor a small church out in the country. He said that he was instructed not to preach past a certain time because if he did, they would "sing him down."

He had no idea what that meant so he asked. He was told that if he preached too long "Mr. So-and-so" would get a hymn-book, call out a hymn number, and the congregation would "sing him down." Can you believe it?

What has happened to us? Are we going to church to truly worship, or are we going out of duty? We have turned away from following God with all of our hearts, and have embraced "new teaching" and "new thinking" that have nothing to do with the word of God. We have embraced our own intellect. Yes, God has allowed our knowledge to increase, but many of us have made little gods out of knowledge and intellect. That's religion—not Christ!

Yes, it's true. Some now go to church for a thrill but not to be eternally changed by the power of Almighty God. Jesus says it's a foolish generation that looks for a sign (Matt. 12:39).

The church is no place for "thrill seekers." Truth seekers, yes, absolutely!

The Ten Commandments have become the Ten Suggestions, and people who call themselves Christians are arguing about the truth of the word of God. We are allowing sin to be practiced among church leaders. We have pulled the covers over our heads. We have compromised what God says is right for the sake of keeping a job. We let the "big givers" in the congregation run the church instead of allowing the Holy Spirit to do His work. We have allowed government to do the job of the church, and our governmental right to religious freedom is threatened every day.

Where is the church? Have we become so much like the world that the world does not recognize us as different? Have we lost our saltiness? We are to be the salt of the earth, the preservers—preserving the word of truth. What has happened? Has the word of God failed? No! The word of God has not failed and it never will (Josh. 23:14).

We have failed. We have compromised. Our disobedience has snuffed out our Light. Our lamp stand is gone (Rev. 2:5).

No one likes to hear about judgement and no one likes to preach judgement. Yet, judgement is a part of the whole counsel of God. If we are to be true worshipers, then we must know what breaks the heart of God. We must repent, agree with God that He is right and that we are wrong, and then be made righteous by submitting our lives again to the lordship of Jesus Christ.

Stop the Sacrifices

God's people, Israel, were in the same mess that I just described above. They had become apathetic toward the word of God and had therefore turned away from truth. They had become religious in their worship, but no love or passion for God was in their hearts.

Because God loved His people, He came to them through the prophet Isaiah with scathing indictment. Isaiah 1:2–3 says, "Listen, O heavens, and hear O earth; for the LORD speaks, 'Sons I have reared and brought up, but they have revolted against me. An ox knows its owner, and a donkey its master's manger, *but* Israel does not know, My people do not understand.'"

This rebuke is to the "sons" of God, people who knew God and at one time had enjoyed a personal relationship with Him. These were heaven-bound people who had lost their passion for God. This is pretty strong, and it's going to get even stronger, so hold on. These verses are not hard to understand; they are just hard to accept.

God is saying that His people are dumber than a donkey. Even a donkey knows and respects the hand that feeds him, but His people have turned away from the One who cares for them. Read this description of their sin: "Alas, sinful nation, people weighed down with iniquity, offspring of evildoers, sons who act corruptly! They have abandoned the LORD, they have despised the Holy One of Israel, they have turned away from Him" (Isa. 1:4).

The word *sinful* means full of lawlessness. Sin is going against the will of God, either by omitting what God's law requires or doing what it forbids! Here it means to miss the mark. Lawlessness can occur in thought (1 John 3:15), in word (Matt. 5:22), or in deed (Rom. 1:32). *Iniquity* here means perverse or twisted or corrupt.

God is saying that His people missed the mark of righteousness and were loaded with the guilt of their sin. They were offspring of evildoers, sons who acted corruptly. This was not the first generation of sinners, but this had been going on for many generations. Their sin was apostasy. They had abandoned, despised, and turned away from the Holy One of Israel.

God had disciplined them before, but they strayed again. God called this waywardness "rebellion." He said they were corrupt from head to toe, inside and out. Their sinfulness was like an opened wound that had not been cared for.

Isaiah 1:5–6 says, "Where will you be stricken again, *as* you continue in *your* rebellion? The whole head is sick, and the whole heart is faint. From the sole of the foot even to the head there is nothing sound in it, *only* bruises, welts, and raw wounds, not pressed out or bandaged, nor softened with oil." Now God points out the result of their sin.

Isaiah 1:7–9: "Your land is desolate, your cities are burned with fire, your fields—strangers are devouring them in your presence; it is desolation, as overthrown by strangers. And the daughter of Zion is left like a shelter in a vineyard, like a watchman's hut in a cucumber field, like a besieged city. Unless the LORD of hosts had left us a few survivors, we would be like Sodom, we would be like Gomorrah" (Isa. 1:7–9).

This is really awful. God says to believers, "Your sin is so bad, I should have destroyed you like I destroyed Sodom and Gomorrah." How many times have you heard someone say that if God does not judge America, He will have to apologize to Sodom and Gomorrah.

Praise God for the remnant! Thank the Lord for the few who hold fast the word of God. Unless the Lord of hosts had left *us* a few survivors, *we* would be like Sodom, *we* would be like Gomorrah?

I am sure that this prophecy flew in the face of all the religious people in Israel at that time. These were not easy words to give; they were not easy words to receive.

Yet these were not the words of the prophet, they were the words of Almighty God. His judgements are righteous.

Let's keep going in Isaiah. In Isaiah 1:10 it says, "Hear the word of the LORD, you rulers of Sodom; give ear to the instruction of our God, you people of Gomorrah."

God identified Israel with Sodom; He called them Gomorrah.

This is horrible. Note that God was addressing the leaders, as well as the people. His words were for everyone.

"'What are your multiplied sacrifices to me?...I have had enough of burnt offerings of rams, and the fat of fed cattle. And I take no pleasure in the blood of bulls, lambs, or goats'" (Isa. 1:11).

Let me rephrase this question for you. God is saying, "What do I think of your worship?" He is going to tell them. God takes no pleasure in their worship! It looks like they have the church-going thing down, but something is very wrong with what they are calling worship. Look! They have multiplied sacrifices, burnt offerings of rams, and the fat of fed cattle. That's a huge offering. What's the problem? Surely if we show up at church and give a huge offering, God will be pleased. But God says He takes no pleasure in it.

I am so thankful that God does not measure our worship by the amount of money we give, raise, or make at a worship event. Worship is measured by the attitude of the heart of the worshiper. God is looking for true worshipers.

And what does God continue to say? "Bring your worthless offerings no longer, incense is an abomination to me. New moon and sabbath, the calling of assemblies—I cannot endure iniquity and the solemn assembly. I hate your new moon *festivals* and your appointed feasts, they have become a burden to me. I am weary of bearing *them*" (Isa 1:13–14).

Stop the sacrifices! Stop coming to church. Stop singing in the choir. Stop the preaching. Stop going to Bible study. Stop giving in the offering. Stop volunteering to be on committees. Just stop! Your offerings are multiplied but they are worthless. Bring them to me no longer. *Stop the sacrifices!*

God told the Israelites that their prayers were an abomination to Him. They wanted God's help, but they had no regard for Him in their hearts. God had had it. He hated their worship and He wanted that aroma to stop ascending to Him!

God hated everything that they called a worship service. He was weary of them. He was tired of their conferences, their "revivals," and all of their gatherings. Their books, their tapes, you name it, He was tired of it. He could not endure their sin (God calls it that) any longer. This is a scathing indictment filled with smoldering indignation.

Now, here comes God's judgement. He is going to answer the question from Isaiah 1:5. "Where will you be stricken again, as you continue in your rebellion?"

Isaiah 1:15 says, "So when you spread out your hands *in prayer*, I will hide My eyes from you, yes, even though you multiply prayers, I will not listen. Your hands are covered with blood."

God said that because they continued in their rebellion, because they continued to abandon the Lord and despised the Holy One of Israel, because they had turned away from Him, He would turn away from them. He would hide His face from them. God was turning His back on Israel. He was not going to answer their prayers, even though they prayed much. They had become a law unto themselves, and God's judgement was to not listen. What hopelessness, what despair!

Our Sin, God's Provision

Nevertheless, God did not leave Israel without hope. He extended an invitation to them to repent. He does the same for us.

There was a call to repentance. God extended an invitation to them once again, to turn from their wicked ways and seek the face of God. They were to come to their senses and not only admit their wrong, but turn away from it and walk in the opposite direction.

Isaiah 1:16–18 says, "Wash yourselves, make yourselves clean; remove the evil of your deeds from My sight. Cease to do evil, learn to do good; seek justice, reprove the ruthless; defend the orphan, plead for the widow. Come now, and let us reason together. Though your sins are as scarlet, they will be as white as snow; though they are red like crimson, they will be like wool."

There was a call to reason. This call was not a call for discussion. It was a call for Israel to evaluate their situation and consider what God had said, and to agree with God that He was right. God's word was to bring about a change of mind, a change of heart. Upon agreeing with God about their sin, God offered them forgiveness and His perfect righteousness.

God's love is unconditional. He will always love us regardless of how we respond to Him. Even when His righteous judgement sentences us to hell, He does so with a broken heart. God loves us, but He is holy and just. No one is destined for hell; we are all destined for righteousness. Refusing God's righteousness, we fit ourselves for hell.

God's forgiveness is absolutely conditional. We receive forgiveness upon our confession and repentance of sin. There is no way around it. We must call right what God calls right, and wrong what God calls wrong. We must agree with God about our sin; there must be a change of heart.

Consider what awaits a repentant heart! The repentant sinner receives the full righteousness of God. A repentant believer receives complete restoration in her relationship with God.

This is where Israel was and where the church is today. Once we see our sin and repent, God will no longer hide His eyes and not listen to our prayers. God will hear us from heaven. He will forgive our sin; He will heal our land.

We need healing in our land today. I have shared the lyric, "Healing comes from knowing who I am." We must know that God is holy, and that God is righteous, and that God is just. He does not change, so if we are to walk in a relationship with Him, *we* must change. He wants to heal us; He wants to help us. Let's allow Him to do just that, by recognizing our sin and repenting and allowing

God to once again restore within us the heart of a true worshiper.

One final warning! "'If you consent and obey, you will eat the best of the land; But if you refuse and rebel, you will be devoured by the sword.' For the mouth of the Lord has spoken" (Isa. 1:19–20).

Worship on God's Terms

My mother always told me that she would spank me right where I "showed out." If I showed out in the street, she would spank me in the street. If I showed out in a store or a restaurant, she would spank me in the store or in the restaurant.

My mother was a teacher, and I went to school with her for four years. My principals and teachers knew my mother's rule. They never had to discipline me. All they had to say was, "Should I ask your mother to come over here?"

I was so afraid that one principal would get my mother, that I wet my pants right there in the hallway! I was in the sixth grade! I was totally humiliated, but it was better than telling my mother.

I wonder if my mom knows about the stuff that I tried to get away with, until someone threatened to tell her. It was very seldom that I got the judgement of mom, because I knew the rules and so did others who took care of me. It was much easier to stop what I was doing than it was to get spanked right where I showed out.

This is what happened to King Uzziah (2 Chron. 26:16–21). He got spanked right where he showed out. In his attempt to show extraordinary zeal and affection for the Lord, he intruded into the temple, beyond where he was allowed. He wanted to burn incense on the altar of the Lord.

It was honorable that the King wanted to worship God by burning incense on the altar, but God had reserved this act of service for the priests, the sons of Aaron. So Uzziah got spanked with a lifelong case of leprosy.

Cain also got spanked where he showed out…in church! It happened to our first parents in the garden, it happened to Israel, and it's happening to many of us today. When we approach God on our terms, we are breaking the rules. His judgement on us is the absence of His presence in our lives. Yes, it's one thing to worship the right God, but it's something else to worship the right God the right way.

Ask God to show you where you have sinned or missed the mark in your life of worship and service to Him. When He shows you, bow the knee to His lordship and allow Him to guide you into a wonderful life of worship. Look again at the lives of Adam, Eve, Cain, King Uzziah, and learn from them how *not* to serve the right God the wrong way!

Consider Philippians 2:3-13 from *The Message* translation:

Agree with each other, love each other, be deep-spirited friends. Don't push your way to the front; don't sweet-talk your way to the top. Put yourself aside, and help others get ahead. Don't be obsessed with getting your own advantage. Forget yourselves long enough to lend a helping hand.

Think of yourselves the way Christ Jesus thought of himself. He had equal status with God but didn't think so much of himself that he had to cling to the advantages of that status no matter what. Not at all. When the time came, he set aside the privileges of being deity and took on the status of a slave, became human! Having become human, he stayed human. It was an incredibly humbling process. He didn't claim special privileges. Instead, he lived a selfless, obedient life and then died a selfless, obedient death—and the worst kind of death at that: a crucifixion.

Because of that obedience, God lifted him high and honored him far beyond anyone or anything, ever, so that all created beings in heaven and on earth—even those long ago

*dead and buried—will bow in worship before this Jesus Christ,
and call out in praise that he is the Master of all, to the glorious
honor of God the Father.*

*What I'm getting at, friends, is that you should simply keep on
doing what you've done from the beginning. When I was living
among you, you lived in responsive obedience. Now that I'm
separated from you, keep it up. Better yet, redouble your efforts.
Be energetic in your life of salvation, reverent and sensitive before
God. That energy is God's energy, an energy deep within you,
God Himself willing and working at what will give him the
most pleasure.*

Watch God Move!

I remember a women's conference where I was asked to lead
worship and provide special music. There were more than three thousand ladies there to worship and fellowship for three days. My job was
to provide all of the music for the five general sessions. The first
one was on a Thursday night.

The session started, and it was my turn to lead the praise and
worship. Of course, I sang with all of my being. But in the middle
of that set, I noticed that I was working really hard. We were
singing wonderful hymns and praise songs, but I felt like I was the
only one excited about them.

I noticed that some women were not singing at all. Some were
even sitting with their arms folded, as if to say, "I am not going to
be a part of this." Some were talking and some were scurrying,
trying to find a seat.

Several things distracted me. The apathy in the singing was
very discouraging. People moving around changed the praise and
worship time to the time to come in and find a seat.

*Personal note: That really gets to me. God has given us music
to open our hearts, and He has given us His word to fill our hearts*

and change our lives. During the opening music is not the time to be finding a seat. Our commitment should be to be seated and prepared for the music when it starts. It's there for us. It's there to help prepare our hearts for the word of God. Next time, don't miss it.

We were also having severe technical problems. The sound and PowerPoint were bad; I thought I was going to die. I wanted nothing more than to leave that stage and never come back.

I recognized that we were under spiritual attack. Once again I was with women who really wanted a movement of God and had prayed diligently for that. They realized that I was struggling and afterward came to talk about what went wrong. I was very honest with them, and the parts they could fix, they did. The other we committed to prayer.

The next session was much better, but still not what we were hoping and praying for. Wonderful speakers like Beth Moore and Esther Burroughs taught us the word of God with power and full conviction. Great Bible teachers from around the state had come in to teach breakout sessions on many different topics. The breakouts were full. The women were getting the word of God.

Our next general session was much more like a general session should be. I remember stopping in the middle of some of the hymns to emphasize the words. They were great, and I did not want the women to miss them. It's easy to sing for the sake of singing, but I wanted us to sing for the sake of worshiping.

I guess they were beginning to realize that the conference was not put together just to give them an outing from home, but that we really were expecting God to change our lives. The women began to focus and the worship soared. The word of God was taught, and there was always time at the end of each session for ladies to respond. I love that. Many times in a worship service the response time is so quick and abrupt that no one responds.

This conference was different. The attenders were allowed all the time they needed to respond, and God did His work.

By the time we got to the last session, the ladies had been taught the word of God for three days, and there really was a different atmosphere in the worship center. However, we really were pushed for time at the last session. Something else was happening in the auditorium and we needed to be out of there *(frustrating)*.

God was in control. He used the events scheduled for that day for His absolute glory. This is what I remember. Author and speaker Esther Burroughs shared Scripture and encouragement. She talked about being empowered by the Holy Spirit. The presence of the Lord entered the building in a powerful way. Esther did not have time to finish.

I was next and wanted to blend together what Esther had shared and what Beth was going to share. I sang what I thought would be most appropriate. The presence of the Lord increased. I could see more than three thousand women beginning to respond from the heart to the presence of the Lord. I did not have time to sing all that I had planned because I wanted to save time for the final speaker.

Beth Moore explained that she had a forty-five minute message with only twenty-five minutes to deliver it. She had prayed and asked God to help her with the message. Beth went on to say that as she was praying, she realized that Esther had shared her first fifteen minutes, and that I had sung her next fifteen minutes, so she had plenty of time to say all that was left for her to say.

The message was powerful. The presence of the Lord was so powerful it was a little frightening. I could hardly wait for Beth to give the invitation. I knew God was about to do an awesome thing. He did.

The minute Beth was finished teaching, it seemed to me like the presence of the Lord rolled over the audience and cleansed the heart of every woman there. There was a breaking in the hearts that only God could do. This time of refreshing truly came from the presence of the Lord.

The call was for repentance, reasoning, and righteousness. The prayer was for a change of heart, aligning with God, and restoration. The altar was filled with repentant hearts, being made whole in the presence of Jehovah. We did indeed fall at His feet like a dead man.

The service ended with:

> *"Change my heart oh God.*
> *Make it ever true.*
> *Change my heart oh God.*
> *May I be like you."*

One eighty-year-old woman, a member of the host church for all her life, looked at the women seeking God and said, "In all my years of coming to church here, I have never seen that many people at this altar."

A mother of a teenager came and thanked the leadership for the conference and the opportunity to truly worship God. With tears in her eyes and a tremble in her voice, she said, "Pray that we don't raise another generation like we were raised."

"Change My Heart Oh God"
(Eddie Espinosa)
© 1982 Mercy/Vineyard Publishing (ASCAP)
Used by permission.

Amazing Grace

Amazing grace how sweet the sound.
That saved a wretch like me.
I once was lost, but now am found.
Was blind, but now I see.

When we've been there
Ten thousand years
Bright shining as the sun
We've no less days
To sing God's praise
Than when we first begun."

"Amazing Grace"
(John Newton)
© 1956 Covington Press
Nashville, Tennessee
All rights Reserved
International Copyright Secured

Chapter Nine

LIFE OF
WORSHIP

SG Ruth Bell Graham tells the story of worrying and praying over someone she loved dearly who was running from the Lord. Awakened in the night, the person came to mind and her imagination began to run wild with fears and concerns. While not audibly, but very certainly, Mrs. Graham soon heard God speaking to her saying, "Quit studying the problems and start studying the promises."

She knew there would be no sleep for her the rest of the night, so she got up, turned on the light and began reading her Bible. She came to the promise in Philippians 4:6–7. "Be anxious for nothing, but in everything by prayer and supplication with thanksgiving let your requests be made known to God. And the peace of God, which surpasses all comprehension, will guard your hearts and your minds in Christ Jesus."

She realized suddenly that the missing ingredient in her prayers was "with thanksgiving." So she put down her Bible and began worshiping God for who He is and thanking God for this loved one and even the difficult spots of life, which taught her so much. Mrs. Graham tells that it was almost as if someone turned the lights on in her mind and heart and those fears and worries seemed smaller. She learned that worship and worry cannot live in the same heart.

Worshiping God brings into proper focus all the worries and concerns of our lives. We discover how great God is and how little we know. When we worship God, our faith is reinforced, our doubts are dissolved, and our joy is restored.

Living a life of worship includes worshiping God in and through the key areas of our lives: home, work, church, and community. It means learning to give attention and affection to God through our relationships, circumstances, and opportunities.

Making Our Home a Place of Worship

My husband and I were excited about the opportunity of seeing our first home built. We were able to choose the colors, wallpaper, carpet, and light fixtures. Initially, we selected the floor plan and what materials we wanted our home to be made out of—brick, stucco, or wood. We looked forward with great anticipation to seeing our red brick home complete. One Friday evening we received a call from the builder telling us they had poured the wrong foundation. Because of an error in paperwork, a foundation for a stucco home had been poured.

We had the option of not accepting the home and starting all over in another neighborhood or accepting this change in the plans for our home. Our only other option was for the builders to add more concrete around and on top of the foundation to make a foundation for a brick home. After deliberating about what to do and talking to those who knew much more than we did about houses, we learned that if we added concrete to the already dry foundation, in the future, if the ground shifted, it could affect our home. Our foundation would not be solid and stabilizing. So, a stucco home it was.

In Matthew 7:24, we read the story of the wise man who built his house on the rock. When the winds blew and the floods came and the storms slammed against the house, it did not collapse and was not destroyed because it was built on a firm foundation.

What foundation is your home built on? I am not talking now about your house, but your home. Is your commitment to Christ the basis for which you live, love, and relate as a family? At the end of the book of Joshua, he challenged the people to choose whom they would serve and live for. He declared to them, "As for me and my house, we will serve the Lord" (Josh. 24:15b). Crisis, loss, pain, suffering, problems, and stresses will happen in our lives and in our families. Yet with Christ as our foundation, the Christian family—the Christian home—will not collapse or be destroyed.

Today, it is hard to give you a picture of a typical home in America. While there are some material possessions that many have in their homes that help them function in the world (telephone, television, computer), family life in our country is as diverse as ever. Families are rich in diversity of nationality, culture, and religion. And the term *family* is no longer reserved for two-parent homes with children.

But some of the statistics about families are troubling. We currently have the highest rate of single parent homes in history. More than three thousand children and teens each day see their parents' marriage end in divorce. Older children, youth, and college-age students are hungry to find a family—a place to belong— that they do not have at home. They are searching to meet this unmet need. Some find family in gangs or in sinful lifestyles. Some turn to the church, but if the church is not prepared to meet their "belonging" needs, they turn elsewhere, confident that the church is a place for adults only or for "people not like them."

The Christian family is confronted with stresses and pressure. It is significant, and perhaps rare, in our culture to worship as family. Even for Christian people, sometimes the hardest place to worship God is in the home. Some families are strangers. Their lives are going too many directions and routines are set that allow for little personal interaction in each other's lives. The sense of belonging in their family is shallow at best.

Sometimes it is difficult to be transparent and honest about spiritual things with our family members because they know us so well. Because we know each other's imperfections, we often feel awkward when we share spiritual things. Family worship can be hindered by the fact that we criticize each other, hold grudges against another, and become frustrated with spouses and children. We allow those things to keep us from sharing and experiencing the presence of God as a family unit in the home.

I encourage you to overcome these obstacles and to work at developing a strong sense of unity and belonging in your family. This sense of belonging will serve as a foundation important for worship. Where there is the knowledge and love of God, His grace can help us to relate to each other in our homes the way He desires. If you have children, the time that you spend together discussing spiritual things, living the Christian life before them, and creating a God-centered atmosphere is important to their spiritual foundation.

In his book *The Family That Makes It*, Ken Anderson says, "Family worship, in its fullest meaning, is not a period of 10, 20, or 30 minutes a day set aside to read and pray together. Family worship, in its most meaningful essence, is the total sum of a father and mother's relationship to each other, to their children, and to God. Family worship relates directly to your disposition in the morning, to your temperament, to the kind of interest you show in your children's activities, to the respect you have for your children's individualities, to the rapport between mother and father."

My parents still live in the home where I grew up in Tennessee. I love to visit them. Recently, I spent some time with them and even stayed there for a weekend when they were away. I told Mark how close I feel to God when I am there. I feel free to be myself, to be creative, and to worship God. Growing up, I didn't give much thought to the gift of Christian parents and the atmosphere they helped to create in our home. They made it very easy for me to sense God, to be aware of Him, and to respond to His work in my life. Now I am extremely grateful to God and to my parents for this foundation. If you are a single parent, single and living alone, or sharing a place with a roommate, it is just as important that you help to nurture and create an atmosphere of worship in your home. As a Christian single, sharing with friends on a spiritual level is important for the health of your Christian life. I encourage you to select a friend or a few friends, with whom you can share and discuss spiritual matters.

During my single days, my roommate and I were able to get an apartment with three bedrooms. We declared our extra bedroom the prayer/music room. This room was reserved for prayer and worship. It was the place we could go for personal devotionals, where I could play my keyboard, where we could be still and be with God. We also had several things around our apartment that we both had acquired on mission trips. We put these items in key places so that when we had visitors and friends at our apartment, we could have natural conversations about our missions and ministry experiences and the purpose of our prayer/music room.

You may be the only Christian in your family. It could be that you are a single mother and trying to raise your children in the love and grace of the Lord. Perhaps, you are married but not to a Christian. You have the challenge of helping your family know about the love of Christ and leading them to develop their own lifestyle of worship. I encourage you to talk with others who share your same situation, give encouragement, and be encouraged by those who find themselves in similar circumstances. Also, let the church and fellow Christian friends help and support you. When the church is acting in the will of God, church members and attendees find a place of family that is bound together by the Spirit of God. The church family helps us grow in Christ and receive the spiritual nurture, fellowship, and support we need.

A five-year-old at our church was talking with adults in the hallway. His mother called to him telling him it was time to go. I heard him say, "Wait, I have to finish talking to my family!" He wanted to talk to his preschool choir teacher before leaving church. His parents and church have helped him understand at an early age that the people of the church are his family, too.

Here are some practical ways that can help you to nurture a lifestyle of worship in your home.

- Have devotional times of worship with family or roommates. Some do it every day, some weekly, others at varying times.

- Pray together as a family.

- Start or continue family traditions to nurture worship as a family, especially in the lives of children.

- Decorate your home with Christian art, pictures, and Scripture verses.

- Place Scripture memory cards around the house—on the bathroom mirror, or at the kitchen sink—in locations that you look at often.

- Attend church together. Pray before going to church or before family members get out of the car after you arrive at church. Pray together for the worship service and for your preparation for and participation in corporate worship.

Worshiping God in the Workplace

We know it is important to have specific times when we engage in focused personal and corporate worship of God. As we develop a lifestyle of worship, we also understand that everything we are and do becomes an expression of worship to God. Our work or vocation is certainly an aspect of our lives that we can offer as worship to Him.

More than any other time in history, women are working and have full-time careers. Our daily jobs encompass much of our lives. If you look around, you will find everything from female bank presidents to symphony conductors. Whether you have a full-time job or are a working full-time wife and mother (or all of the above), your life's work can be expressed as worship unto God.

Colossians 3:23 says "Whatever your task, put yourselves into it, as done for the Lord and not for your masters." This has been a favorite verse of mine since I was a teenager. Whatever you do, do it for the Lord. We know the Lord deserves our best. God is honored in excellence, in a job well done. How can you worship God through your work? By doing your best job, by serving Him and others with excellence, and by relating to others as Christ would relate to them.

The majority of us encounter other people in our work—co-workers, clients, customers, employees, and employers. Each day that we serve and work with them, we have the God-given opportunity to relate to them with the love and attitude of Christ. Often our pride gets in the way and our personal success, our wants and desires, become more important than being a servant of Christ. Scripture is clear that we are called to be servants. Our lives should be different than those who are not Christ-followers, and those whom we work with should notice. "But thanks be to God, who always leads us in triumph in Christ, and manifests through us the sweet aroma of the knowledge of Him in every place" (2 Cor. 2:14). Do others see Jesus in you at your workplace? Is the sweet aroma of Christ something others sense in your life?

As we are examples of who Christ is to the world, the character of Christ should be evident in all our dealings, relationships, and actions. Some of the greatest damage to the cause of Christ has come by those who say they are Christians, but in their work are dishonest, who disregard the importance of Christian integrity, and fail to consider whom they are serving no matter what or whom they encounter.

How can our work or vocation become an expression of worship? By doing exactly what Romans 12:1–2 tells us, by offering our lives to God as a living sacrifice, allowing God to work through us, transform us, help us with our weaknesses, use our strengths, and glorify Himself through our lives.

Perhaps your work atmosphere is much less than a Christian environment. Let me encourage you, God wants to use you there in that place. God wants to "manifest the sweet aroma of God" all through that place. While your workplace may seem full of spiritual darkness and complacency, God can and wants to use you for great purposes in His kingdom as you give each day of your work to Him.

Whether you are in a non-Christian environment or a Christian environment, the importance of praying for your co-workers, clients, or customers cannot be underestimated. As you pray for your own work, for those around you, and those you come in contact with, you are participating in the work of God. It is not your responsibility to change or transform others. That is God's work. But He wants to use you to be a part of it as you stay in constant communion with Him. First Thessalonians 5:17 says, "Pray without ceasing." God will honor your praying without ceasing, at and for your workplace.

Whatever your career, it is important to have Christian fellowship, encouragement, and accountability. Perhaps you work with other Christians. If so, you should be a support to each other. If you do not, I encourage you to find a small group of Christian women with whom you can share your Christian life. The prayer support and accountability with other Christian women will be a strength to you as you seek to give your work and all of life to the Lord each day. As we give our lives to God in worship, our priorities will be aligned with His. Our daily work and service will be an expression of worship, giving glory to Him at all times.

Worshiping God in our Community/World

When your neighbors pass your house, do they know that Christians live there? Just as in our workplace people need to recognize that there is something unique about us—the sweet aroma of the knowledge of God. Our neighbors and those we encounter in our community and world need to sense this, as well. A lifestyle of worship will express itself in Christlike concern for the community and world. An awareness of the lost world, human suffering, and need will grow in us as we draw closer to God in honesty and sincerity.

The book of Acts tells the exciting days of the early beginnings of the Christian church. The early Christians met together to worship, to hear the apostles' teaching, to fellowship, and to share meals. They sold their possessions and goods and gave to anyone who had need. They sacrificed for each other and were quick to take care of each other.

Worship transforms us, and a lifestyle of worship is one that has a concern for the world around them. As we are changed and shaped by God, He develops His life in us. We look at others with God's eyes and begin to see as He sees. We recognize the needs that He is concerned about meeting, and in many cases, He uses us to meet those needs.

As God's people, His true worshipers, our lives should be a light to others that points to Christ. We are light in the darkness, and we should shine brightly so that others can see Him in us. Jesus tells us we are the light of the world and our light shines as others see our good deeds. The result? Matthew 5:16 says others who see those good deeds will "praise our Father in heaven."

A lifestyle of worship is contagious. As people seek purpose and meaning in life, they will find the truth in you! People in your community may be going through crisis or difficulty and God can use you to bring His love and truth to them. A lifestyle of worship is contagious because it fulfills our purpose for living: to worship and enjoy God forever. Others will discover their purpose as they see in you what it means to know God and live a lifestyle that worships Him.

Being a True Worshiper at God's House

One Sunday, during the time of writing this book, I arrived at Sunday School to find the title of our lesson was *Renewing Your Worship*. We discussed the importance of our heart's motives in worship, the importance of recognizing who God is, and not just going through the motions disconnected to the fact that God is present.

In the worship service, our pastor's sermon focused on Romans 12:1–2, a passage that has become significant to me in the last few years with its focus on offering our daily lives to God as an act of worship. That night I led the college Bible study on— you guessed it—worship. The focus passage for our Bible study was John 4. The message of worship was everywhere I turned.

That was a day of continuation in my journey to learn to be a true worshiper of God. I believe God was continuing to teach me about worship and even enabling me to write words for this book. One of the important things we discussed throughout all these experiences of the day was the importance of being honest with God in both our personal and corporate worship. We also emphasized doing our part to connect with God—to prepare ourselves spiritually, mentally, and physically for the experience of corporate worship.

Ginger Smith is a twenty-something who has committed her life to reaching the "down and outs" with the love of Jesus. She spends much of her life's energy on helping the homeless, those with substance addictions, the abused, and the lonely in the inner city of New Orleans. Ginger serves the Lord on a daily basis and is helping those she comes in contact with to know the love of God.

On one occasion, Ginger shared with me how this ministry and work can be draining and how important her times of worship (both personal and corporate) are for her effectiveness in ministry. She also shared (not knowing I would later write about it) how important it is for her to prepare herself for corporate worship. As she drives to church, she plays music that will help her to begin to focus on God rather than all the problems of the world and those with whom she ministers. She uses the time to get prepared to come before God with her local fellowship of Christian believers.

I recently asked some worship leaders who serve in local churches what they believed was one of the things that people need most to hear or understand about worship. They responded that a desperate need exists for people to understand the importance of preparing themselves for corporate worship. Many people do not even think about being ready for worship before they arrive at church.

When we come together with other Christian believers, we are approaching our Almighty and Holy God. Do you take that for granted? We walk into the church sanctuary or worship center and sit down, almost as if we are watching TV or a movie, expecting to be entertained. We gaze, we watch, we hope to enjoy it, and maybe even get something out of it for ourselves. But we have made no effort to meet with our Living God. We sit, stand, sing, smile, and leave…never having truly worshiped God.

James Christensen, Christian minister of more than thirty years and author of *Don't Waste Your Time in Worship,* once wrote of his conviction that many people who attend church do not worship God at all. He believes they waste their time. There are more spectators than participants and more persons seeking religious entertainment than seeking to worship God. They are completing a hurried visit where they are distracted, rather than communing with God.

Our hurried lives and busy schedules fill us to overflowing, and we are unable to have a childlike faith that Jesus affirms. Our "sin of hurry" keeps us from giving our attention and worship to God. We can't help but be distracted. God wants us to find our rest and peace and purpose in Him. St. Augustine reminds us that our soul will never rest until it finds its rest in God.

I haven't even mentioned what takes place in the typical Christian home on Sunday before going to church. We argue and complain, and the rush to look our best takes priority. Before we ever arrive we are frazzled, frustrated, and not even close to being in an attitude of worship.

In her book *Making Sunday Special*, Karen Burton Mains gives ten practical suggestions for preparing your heart for Sunday. These Saturday exercises take very little time, but can be very helpful as you seek to prepare yourself for the next day's worship. She suggests trying one a week and finding out the worship theme or focus of the Sunday sermon earlier in the week. I suggest that you also lead your children and youth to try some of these exercises.

1. Write a short letter to God, as you might write to a friend. Express how, as you walk with God, you see that He is characterized by a certain attribute. In essence, this will be a written prayer. When you finish the letter, read it aloud to God.

2. Set aside fifteen minutes on Saturday for a time of private adoration. Think about God. If you are praising Him as all powerful, you may see Him seated on a throne. If you are praising Him for his love, you might imagine Christ on the cross.

Then choose a posture appropriate for this mental picture: sitting, kneeling, walking together. Once you have done this, tell Christ how pleased you are that He is characterized by the worship theme of that given Sunday.

3. Choose a song that expresses your praise to God. Through meditation, allow this music to capture your heart.

4. Think about God's work in your life. Who has God proven Himself to be for you? Now share your thoughts with someone else. Complete this exercise by thanking the Lord for the privilege of telling another of His worth.

5. Look for a passage of Scripture that underscores a worship theme. You might want to choose verses from several parts of the Bible, much like you would if you were preparing a responsive reading. Tell God, "These verses are from You, but I also read them to You." Then read them out loud to the Lord. You might do this as a prayer before your Saturday evening meal.

6. The psalmist often affirms God by reviewing how He worked in the past. Spend time looking back on your life. How has the Lord already proven Himself to you? Write down on a sheet of paper at least five personal incidents that convince you He is worthy of your praise.

7. Spend fifteen minutes talking with a friend or family member about the Lord. Welcome Christ into your conversation as you remember His promise to be present when even two or three have gotten together in His name. Discuss together how Christ has proven Himself in your lives.

8. Poetry has often been used by God's people to express their adoration and praise. If you are gifted in this way, write something original. If not, find a poem that reflects a worship theme. Take the poem with you to church to silently read to the Lord in the quiet before the service.

9. Adoration can sometimes be shown through gifts given to the Lord or to someone else on His behalf. In such a case one's prayer is:

"Lord, this special gift is given as a way of expressing my praise to you. Accept it, I pray, as from the heart of one who loves you. Amen."

10. Come up with an original way to express praise to God as you prepare yourself for church tomorrow.[1]

God is concerned with our hearts. He is interested in our motives for bringing offerings. In Malachi 1:1–10, the people were unable to worship because they had no reverence, respect, or appreciation for who God was. The people brought defiled offerings before God.

God wants our best. He deserves our best. God is worthy of all worship. Revelation 5:13 says, "To Him who sits on the throne, and to the Lamb, be blessing and honor and glory and dominion forever and ever." How can we bring, give, or offer our best worship to God when we have not even considered what we are doing?

Preparation is vital for meaningful, true worship to occur. We must come before God with pure motives and complete trust in who He is. He is delighted, worshiped, and glorified when we offer Him our best.

Do you seek to give your best to God in all you do and are? Do you offer God your best attention, energy, focus, and time? Do you take time to prepare for worship, both personal and corporate? Has your worship life simply included going to church because you live in a social culture that expects you to? If you do not consider whom you are worshiping and what you are doing, then God is not being honored or worshiped. You are most likely living a powerless Christian life.

I recently had a discussion with a seminary professor and worship leader who said, "I am convinced that our churches will grow, not because of good preaching or good music, but only because of our worship." When the church is expressing true worship, God's Spirit is free to move, work, and change lives. Others will sense the Spirit of God alive and active and will be drawn to the truth of who God is and His love for them.

Several years ago Steve Green, a Christian recording artist, recorded a song called "The Mission." A phrase from that song has stayed with me for it describes the essence of the importance of worship and the place of service and ministry in our lives. "To love the Lord, our God, is the heartbeat of our mission. The strength from which our service overflows."

Our love for God is the foundation from which our Christian service flows. Often dedicated Christians fall prey to the idea that because they are doing good works they are worshiping God. Consider the fine line here; good deeds do not equal true worship. Doing things for God is not worship if the actions are not motivated by our love for God and our relationship with Him.

When we examine the life of Jesus, we see how the needs that He saw and wanted to meet were, at times, overwhelming. Yet, because of Christ's relationship with His Father, He was able to do what was necessary and discern what was best. Most importantly, He never lost the fresh commitment to loving and following God. We need to be careful that our relationship with God is active, alive, and growing. We must take the time to express our love and worship to God each day. Our involvement in ministry should be compelled by our love relationship with God and not by any other thing. ▧

---

[1] Mains, Karen Burton, *Making Sunday Special* (Wheaton: Mainstay Church Resources, n.d.), 106-107. Used by permission.

I Will Follow You
Sarah S. Groves

With everything inside me, with all my heart and soul,
With all my mind and passion, and everything I know,
I will follow You, until the whole world knows
That God is love and in Him there is hope.

I will follow You, I will lift up my voice
I will sing Your praise forever, In You I will rejoice.
I will follow You, until the whole world knows,
That God is love and in Him there is hope.

Give Me Your Eyes
Sarah S. Groves

Give me Your eyes to see the needs around me.
Give me Your eyes to see the pain.
Give me Your eyes to understand others.
Give me Your eyes so that I don't live in vain.

Chapter Ten

Worship—The Eternal Experience

Recently, I had a discussion with my eighty-nine-year-old grandmother about the end of time. A lifelong, faithful, daily Bible reader, she has examined much of what the book of Revelation has to say about this. The end of time has become more of a subject of interest, probably because she is in the later years of her life. I'll be honest with you; some things about the last days cause me to be afraid. My fear is more of the unknown, than about where I will end up. It could be that I have a tainted impression or understanding because of what I have heard others say about the end of time.

One thing of which I am certain is that I will be forever in eternity with my God. And from everything I understand in Scripture, the purpose for our creation—to worship, love, and enjoy God forever—begins here on earth. We will spend eternity praising, blessing, worshiping, and enjoying God's presence forever. The life we know now is just the beginning! We are learners, students, disciples of Jesus Christ. As we know Him now, even more will we know Him in eternity. "For now we see in a mirror dimly but then face to face; now I know in part, but then I will know fully just as I also have been fully known" (1 Cor. 13:12).

Philippians 2:9–11 says, "Therefore also God highly exalted Him, and bestowed on Him the name which is above every name, so that at the name of Jesus every knee will bow, of those who are in heaven and on earth and under the earth, and that every tongue will confess that Jesus Christ is Lord, to the glory of God the Father." As Christian believers, we do not live as those without hope, but as those with assurance that after this life on earth, we will be forever in eternity with God. And at some point every person will confess that Jesus Christ is Lord and will bow down in worship before Him.

When we examine the book of Revelation, we see powerful expressions of worship that will occur in heaven. These worship experiences help us see the right standing of our relationship with God. He is immortal God and we are mortal human beings. Yet, because of His great love for us, He has given us the ability to worship Him now. While these words indicate what is to come, as true worshipers, we do not have to wait to express our worship in the ways that these passages indicate.

In Revelation 4:9–11 we discover people who "give glory and honor and thanks to Him." We see people falling down before Him and worshiping Him. The people say "Worthy are You, our Lord and our God, to receive glory and honor and power; for You created all things and because of Your will they existed and were created."

In Revelation 5:11–14, the worship description is powerful: "Angels, living creatures, myriads of myriads, thousands of thousands saying with a loud voice, 'Worthy is the Lamb that was slain to receive power and riches and wisdom and might and honor and glory and blessing.' And every created thing which is in heaven and on the earth and under the earth and on the sea, and all the things in them,... saying, 'To Him who sits on the throne, and to the Lamb, be blessing and honor and glory and dominion forever and ever.' and others...kept saying 'Amen'...and fell down and worshiped Him."

In the great musical work *The Messiah* by George Handel, there is a section where the full choir sings with full voice, "Blessing and Honor, Glory and Power, be unto the Lamb." I have had the privilege of singing this renowned composition on several occasions with large choirs and orchestras. One experience in particular allowed for a three-hundred-voice choir and large orchestra. Many different countries were represented there. As we sang with full voice and sound, I felt I got just a tiny glimpse of what it is going to be like when "myriads and myriads, thousands and thousands" declare their worship and give blessing, honor, glory, and power to the living God.

By God's grace we are getting a glimpse of who He is as we live on this earth. He longs for us to know Him and love Him and worship Him with all that we are. He promises that when we seek Him, we will find Him. God also promises that we can experience the fullness of His love and an abundant life as we follow Him. This fullness and abundance is just a glimpse of what is yet to come.

True worshipers, God is calling us to give our fullest attention, our greatest affection, and the totality of who we are to Him. May we know Him more and respond to His Truth. Let us celebrate, shout for joy, lift holy hands, for one day we will worship Him face-to-face. Amen!

Welcome Home

Sarah S. Groves

"Welcome home," said the parent to the child. "I have waited long for this day."

With arms outstretched, a huge embrace, there was so much they wanted to say

Battle scars and hurts and pains, all part of the child's journey home,

Erased and eased by the Father's love, "Welcome home, child, welcome home."

"Forever we will enjoy this gift and love each other well.

I with you and you with me, we've many stories to tell.

I watched as you struggled and found your way to Me."

The child bowed down in love for Him, in true humility.

The greatness, power, and glory of God, now seen face to face

The response of the child so clear and true, it was an experience of Grace.

Worship, praise, adoration, love expressed forever now

Joining the host of others who before the King do bow.

The King of Kings, the Lord of Lords, His glory to behold,

Eternity with God, enjoying Him forever,
"Welcome home, child, welcome home."

SUGGESTIONS FOR WORSHIP

EXPRESSIONS OF WORSHIP

Prayer
Music
Listening
Singing
Playing instruments
Reading Scripture/Promises
Dancing
Clapping
Shouting
(Possible words to shout- Hallelujah or Amen)
Being in Nature and Beauty and recognizing God
who is Creator of all
Expressing our Emotions
Tears
Laughter
Body Language
Standing at attention
Kneeling
On your face
Bowing
On knees
Hands lifted up
Hands Open/Raised
Lord's Supper/Eucharist
Hearing the word preached/taught
Hearing and sharing personal testimonies

GOD IS...

1. **Omniscient**—Knows all

   Psalm 139:1–6

2. **Omnipotent**—All powerful

   Genesis 18:14

   Jeremiah 32:27

3. **Omnipresent**—Ever present

   Proverbs 15:3

   Jeremiah 23:24

4. **Eternal**—No beginning, no end

   Deuteronomy 32:40

   Isaiah 57:15

5. **Immutable**—Never changes

   Psalm 102:27

   Malachi 3:6

   Hebrews 13:8

6. **Incomprehensible**—Beyond man's understanding

   Job 11:7

   Romans 11:33

7. **Self-Existent**—Depends on nothing beyond himself for His existence

   Exodus 3:14

   John 5:26

8. **Self-Sufficient**—Brings about His will without the aid of anyone

   Psalm 50:12

9. **Infinite**—Has no limits

   1 Kings 8:27

   Psalm 145:3

10. **Transcendent**—Exists totally apart from creation

    Isaiah 55:8-9

11. **Sovereign**—Supreme ruler over all

    Daniel 4:35

12. **Holy**—Morally excellent/Perfect

   Leviticus 19:2

   Job 34:10

13. **Righteous**—Always does what is right

   Deuteronomy 32:4

   Psalm 119:142

14. **Just**—Completely fair

   Numbers 14:18

   Psalm 89:14

15. **Merciful**—Actively compassionate

   Psalm 62:12

   Psalm 89:14

   Psalm 106:44-45

   Psalm 116:5

   Romans 9:14-16

16. **Long-suffering**—Slow to anger/His anger is righteous

   Numbers 14:18

   2 Peter 3:9

17. **Wise**—All wise

   Isaiah 40:28

   Daniel 2:20

18. **Loving**—Unconditional love

   Jeremiah 31:3

   Romans 5:8

   1 John 4:8

19. **Good**—No evil exists in Him

   2 Chronicles 5:13

20. **Wrathful**—Hates unrighteousness

   Exodus 34:6-7

   Romans 1:18

21. **Truthful**—Every word God speaks is absolute truth

   Psalm 31:5

   Psalm 119:160

   Titus 1:2

22. **Faithful**—True to His promises

   Deuteronomy 7:9

   2 Timothy 2:13

23. **Jealous**—Unwilling to share what is rightfully His

   Exodus 20:5

   Exodus 34:14

Developing a Lifestyle of Worship

If you haven't already, make Christ Lord of your life. Make knowing God your first priority. As you do this, you will be able to give yourself completely over to Him and put your full trust, attention, and affection in Him.

- **Get to know God.**
  - ~ Spend time with Him…just you and Him…alone with Him.
  - ~ Spend time in His word. Study it, know and understand it. Apply it to your life.
  - ~ Spend time in prayer.
  - ~ Commune with God. Have two-way communication with Him. Talk, cry, laugh, and share with Him. Listen to what God wants to say to you. Ask Him to speak, to direct, to lead.
  - ~ Wait with Him. Worship Him.

- **Worship and fellowship with other Christians.**
  - ~ Spend time with other Christians. Learn from others. Allow God to strengthen the unity of sisters and brothers in Christ. Share, study God's word, and pray with other Christians.
  - ~ Worship with other Christians. "Don't forsake the assembling together" (Heb. 10:25). Corporate worship is as important as personal worship, but the two can't be separated. Your corporate worship is enhanced because you experience personal worship. Your personal worship is enhanced because of your corporate worship experiences.

- **Take care of yourself.**
  - ~ Fitness or wellness of the whole person is important. Jesus teaches us this through the example of His life (Luke 2:52).
  - ~ Take care of your physical body with proper nutrition, exercise, and rest.
  - ~ Take care of your mind by learning new things.
  - ~ Take care of relationships in your life.

- **Worship with all you are!**
  - ~ As you do these things, cultivate your worship of God. Bring all that you are before the Lord—your heart, mind, soul, strength and worship Him, respond to His Truth, with your full attention and affection.

A Model for Personal Worship and Devotion

1. Spend several minutes in stillness and silence. Begin to focus on God and allow any distractions, both outward and inward, to be put aside. Recognize the importance of being sincere and honest with God.

2. As you focus your thoughts on God, choose a Scripture, perhaps a psalm or a verse in Psalms, about God's character to help you concentrate on Him.

3. Spend some moments in prayer and praise. Worship God and come before Him with adoration and praise. Express your love to Him. Get in a physical posture that will help you to express your worship to God. (Sit, stand, get on your knees, raise your hands, bow, etc.) Use some of the words listed under "God Is" above to express your worship, if this is helpful.

4. Sing a song of worship. You may want to choose a hymn or chorus that has great meaning to you and gives worship to God. Another option is to play one recorded song that helps you to worship.

5. Acknowledge God's greatness and your dependence on Him. Confess any sin and receive God's forgiveness.

6. Read Scripture and choose a verse that you want to focus on and memorize.

7. Pray and bring your life before God. Seek His will and desire for Your life. Pray specifically and listen to what God wants to say to you. Take time in silence and meditation after you pray to listen for God's voice. Focus your mind's attention and heart's affection on God. Wait before Him and worship Him. ❧